Football Jokes

Football Jokes

350 Hilarious Quips, Zingers, and Belly Laughs

TOM ROCK

Sports Publishing books may be purchased in bulk at special discounts for sales promotion, corporate gifts, fund-raising, or educational purposes. Special editions can also be created to specifications. For details, contact the Special Sales Department, Sports Publishing, 307 West 36th Street, 11th Floor, New York, NY 10018 or sportspubbooks@skyhorsepublishing.com.

Sports Publishing® is a registered trademark of Skyhorse Publishing, Inc.®, a Delaware corporation.

Visit our website at www.sportspubbooks.com.

10 9 8 7 6 5 4 3 2 1

Library of Congress Cataloging-in-Publication Data is available on file.

Front cover design by David Ter-Avanesyan
Front cover and interior illustrations by Rich Harris

Print ISBN: 978-1-68358-494-0
Ebook ISBN: 978-1-68358-495-7

Printed in China

To Amanda

for always laughing, at jokes or otherwise.

Table of Contents

Introduction

Here's a true story . . .

Hakim Laws of Philadelphia had just become a hero. Then he became a legend. The Philadelphia man saved several children from a burning building in 2019 after he noticed flames coming out of a second-story apartment building window. "I see a guy hanging out the window screaming that his kids were in there," Laws told TV cameras after the incident. "My man just started throwing babies out the window, and we was catching them—unlike Agholor, and his mishaps. I'd like to put that out there."

The reference was to Eagles receiver Nelson Agholor, who had dropped several passes already that season.

It reminded me of a joke I'd heard when I was younger, the one about a former NFL wide receiver who became a fireman.

One day, still relatively new on the job, he was called to a burning building. High up in one of the windows a woman was shouting, "My baby! My baby!" and holding her infant out the window. The firefighter yelled up, "Don't worry, ma'am! I was an NFL receiver! I can catch anything!"

Desperate, she dropped her child and it came spiraling down, down, down toward the ground. Sure enough, the firefighter caught it softly in his hands. The child cooed, unaware of its harrowing adventure.

"Just like the old days!" the firefighter said.

Everyone around him began to clap and cheer—until he celebrated the catch with a touchdown spike.

There is nothing inherently funny about football. It is a serious game played by serious people for serious stakes. But every so often, the sport contorts itself into a vehicle for the comical and the inane, for the quirky and the silly, the laughably clever and the laughably not-so-clever.

This book is a collection of just a few such glimpses behind the violent tackles and dazzling athletic feats that we watch unfold with awe every season. Some are absolutely true, like the Agholor one, while others, like the overzealous firefighter, are so far-fetched they are completely detached from reality. Some may elicit groans, others belly laughs, and still more knowing chuckles.

Together, they illustrate a brighter side of the sport of football.

Only around 348 or so more to go! And when you are done reading all of them, feel free to celebrate by spiking this book like a touchdown.

Strange Stories, Part I

Some sports radio callers really know how to multitask! In 2023 an Eagles fan who identified himself as "Peter from Lehigh Valley" called into WIP in Philadelphia to rail about the Cowboys a few days before an NFC East game against the Eagles.

"I have never hated anything more than the Dallas Cowboys, ever," Peter said passionately. "The only game I look forward to any year, 365 days, all four major sports, is the Dallas–Eagles game in Philly. We need to bring this back. I hate the Cowboys. Everyone who loves the Eagles should hate the Cowboys, including the players."

He then implored Eagles coach Nick Sirianni to tap into that regional distaste.

"Sirianni is a motivator, he's all about culture," Peter continued. "He needs to bring that back. He's gotta get the team up, the players up, to hate the Cowboys, hit them in the face, knee them in the glory holes as Jerry [Jones, the owner of the Cowboys] would say."

All of a sudden, as Peter continued to rant, a police siren could be heard in the background of the call.

Was he being stopped by the cops? Nope.

"Sorry," Peter said calmly, "I'm pulling someone over."

Turns out Peter *was* the cops! And not even tracking down speeders on the highway would stop him from sharing his thoughts on the Eagles!

"This could be the division!" Peter continued with his train of thought after the brief aside to attend to police matters. "This could be home-field advantage for the playoffs or not!"

The radio hosts, Joe Giglio and Hugh Douglas, were flabbergasted by Peter's ability to juggle his professional responsibilities with his sports passion.

"We officially have my new favorite caller," Giglio said after Peter hung up and, presumably, went back to work.

Hopefully, the guy he pulled over wasn't a Cowboys fan.

Coaches are supposed to be the level-headed purveyors of calm on the sidelines. No one told that to Houston Oilers defensive coordinator Buddy Ryan and offensive coordinator Kevin Gilbride in 1993, though.

After a season of public bickering over strategies (Ryan did not like Gilbride's insistence on throwing the ball late in games), the two coaches got into a sideline altercation in the regular-season finale against the Jets. It began when the Oilers, leading 14–0 late in the half, fumbled a snap and gave the ball back to the Jets. Ryan stormed over to Gilbride to complain about the aggressive play calling, harsh animated words were exchanged between the two, and—pow!—Ryan threw a punch straight to Gilbride's jaw.

Even after tempers cooled, the animosity between the two did not. A few days after the incident, Ryan said, "Kevin Gilbride will be selling insurance in two years."

Gilbride actually went on coach sixteen more seasons—including the following year in Houston!—winning two Super Bowls as offensive coordinator of the Giants.

Players get busted at airports with all manner of illegal and illicit things. Yet few create the kind of hubbub that Vikings running back Onterrio Smith stirred in 2005, when he was caught traveling with a product called, "The Original Whizzinator."

What exactly is a Whizzinator, you may ask? Well, it is an elaborate contraption designed to beat drug tests that comes with clean, dried urine, a bladder, a jock strap, a heating element, and a fake penis.

Using the device during an NFL drug test was (obviously) a violation of league drug policies, and while Smith told police he was taking the vials to his cousin, he was eventually suspended by the NFL. He never played again.

There are plenty of times and places when football metaphors can be useful. Matthew Merryman, a Kansas City attorney, chose to dive headlong into the sport's vernacular as his client pled guilty to a string of bank robberies and faced fifty years in federal prison.

Xaviar Michael Babudar, who was known as the superfan "ChiefsAholic," dressing as a wolf for most Chiefs home games, became infamous when he was arrested in December 2022 for a bank robbery in Oklahoma. He then skipped out on bail that March and was added to Kansas City's Most Wanted list in June. He was arrested by the FBI in July on nineteen charges around six bank robberies across four states, other failed robberies, money laundering, and more.

After Babudar pled guilty to three charges in February 2024, Merryman faced the media and gave a Knute Rockne–esque summation of the situation:

“From the beginning of this case, folks, the government has been blitzing. And Xaviar’s pocket was collapsing. But today, Xaviar has stepped into the pressure. He took responsibility for his actions. He stood up in court humble and repentant, and admitted what he had done.

“Now, if I know anything about Xaviar, and if the Chiefs Kingdom knows anything about ChiefsAholic, we know that he doesn’t give up. We know that if he stumbled, and he fell, he didn’t let his knee touch the ground. And that’s because he’s capable of doing a great thing.

“He knows that there’s still hope. We still have a lot of work to do on this case, but Xaviar wants everyone to know that he loves Chiefs Kingdom, he loves Kansas City, and he hopes that you’ll rally to his support.”

Game balls are typically given out for result-changing plays. Larry Izzo, a former Patriots special teamer, earned one for a very different reason: He had to poop during a game and, instead of retreating to the locker room to take care of business, he “went for two” in a bucket on the sideline. That his “Super Bowel” escapade went unnoticed by the thousands of fans and dozens of cameras surrounding the field was enough to impress coach Bill Belichick.

“This is 100 percent true,” teammate Wes Welker said on ESPN in 2012. “And Larry would be so mad at me if I said that this didn’t happen, because he takes ultimate pride in this whole deal. Of all the special teams tackles and Pro Bowls he’s made, I guarantee you that game ball is probably a more prized item for him than his Super Bowl rings.”

Asked to explain the logistics of the endeavor, however, Welker was thankfully shy on details.

"It's Izzo, it's what the guy does!" Welker said. "I'm telling you, the guy is phenomenal."

Seahawks wide receiver DK Metcalf is far less surreptitious than Izzo about his scatological urges. In fact, in 2022, he needed to be carted off the field and into the locker room in the middle of a game against the Lions to take care of his business.

Metcalf told the story on the *Up & Adams Show*:

"So, this is the middle of the drive and I come out for a play, and I told my receivers coach, I was like, 'Hey, I gotta go to the bathroom.' He was like, 'You got to pee or do a number two?' I said, 'I gotta do a number two.' And then it went away for like 10 seconds, so I was like, all right, I'll go back in the game.

"And when I was back in the game the feeling came back up. So we ended up scoring like two plays later, and so I run back to the sideline and they had a cart ready for me.

"The head trainer was like, 'You got to go to the bathroom?' I was like, 'Yeah.' He was like, 'There's a cart down there.' I'm like, 'Bro, I'm not taking a cart.' So then the equipment manager comes up and was like, 'Hey, there's a cart down there, I think you should go ahead and go.'

"If anybody's played in Detroit, they know it is a long-ass walk from the locker room to the field. And I was not gonna make that walk, by far, no, was not going to make it. That clinch walk wasn't going to make it.

"Pete [Carroll, the Seahawks head coach] wanted me to do it on the sideline," Metcalf added. "Pete was like, if Larry [Izzo] can do it, you can do it . . . I'm like, 'No, I got too much respect for myself, I can't, I can't do it on the sideline.' And so I hopped on the cart and went to the locker room."

Jokey Jokes, Part I

Quarterback Andy Aches took another hard sack, managed to get to his feet, and made his way to the huddle.

"Knock, knock," Andy said when he finally regained the ability to speak.

"Who's there?" his offensive linemen responded.

"Zany."

"Zany who?"

"Zany body going to block that guy?"

What is black and white but never right? A referee.

What did the coach say to the mummy at the end of practice? Let's wrap this up.

What's the difference between a nickel defense and a dime defense? Five cents.

Why didn't the football team want to play in the jungle? There were too many cheetahs.

Old quarterbacks never die. They just pass away.

Did you hear about the two quarterbacks who didn't get along? They were both too passive aggressive.

Why does Switzerland's football team always get penalized? They line up in the neutral zone.

Where do NFL teams get their unforms each year? New Jersey.

Did you know some of the very best football players are actually two-sport athletes? They are Pro Bowlers, too.

Why was the dog kicked out of the football league? He kept ruffing the passer.

What impressed the coaches most about their new kicker? He put his best foot forward.

Why did the football team recruit an airline pilot? Because he kept making touchdowns.

Why did the quarterback go to the Italian restaurant before the game? To fill up on pass-ta.

Why did the team bring a ladder to its last game? Because it heard the championship was up for grabs.

Why did the opposing team bring a ladder, too? Because they heard the stakes were high.

How do football players stay warm in the winter? They huddle up.

Why did the football prefer the punter to the placekicker? Because the punter didn't kick him when he was down.

After years of a strict uniform code, Coach Callous let his players inscribe their cleats with short, personalized messages. Most decided to put inspirational phrases on their shoes or the initials of their girlfriend. Billy Blockhead wrote "T.G.I.F." on his.

"I like it," Coach Callous said. "Thank God It's Friday. We should all be focused on the games on Friday nights. Good job, Billy."

"Coach, that's not what it means," Billy said.

"Well," Coach Callous replied, "why else would you write T.G.I.F. on your cleats?"

"It's a reminder," Billy said. "Toes Go In First."

Gridiron Gaffes

Jim Marshall had, by any measure, a very successful NFL career. He played 20 seasons, made two Pro Bowls, and was a key member of the Vikings' "Purple People Eaters" defense in the 1970s.

But the play he is most known for is one he'd surely rather forget . . . and one of the most embarrassing moments any player has faced on the field.

On October 25, 1964, playing in San Francisco, the Vikings led, 27–17, in the fourth quarter. The game seemed settled, especially when the 49ers coughed up the ball in their own territory and Marshall, the 6-foot-4, 260-pound Vikings defensive end, recovered it. Marshall started off running toward with the ball toward the end zone.

The *wrong* end zone!

Everyone knew what was going on except Marshall, including a disbelieving play-by-play announcer, who said that Marshall "is running the wrong way" and "thinks he's scored a touchdown."

Upon arriving in his end zone all by himself, Marshall tossed the ball in a nonchalant celebration. A 49ers player rushed up, patted Marshall on the arm, and said, "Thanks, Jim." The referees awarded San Francisco two points for a safety.

Very fortunately for Marshall, the Vikings held on in that game, winning 27–22.

Everyone thought speedy Eagles receiver DeSean Jackson had scored his first NFL touchdown in a *Monday Night Football* game against the Cowboys in 2008.

He did not.

After catching a 61-yard pass from Donovan McNabb and cruising past the defenders on his way to the end zone, Jackson got a little ahead of himself and threw the ball down in celebration before he actually crossed the goal line. While the play was initially ruled a touchdown on the field, the Cowboys challenged the call and replays showed that Jackson had, in fact, lost control of the ball before scoring. Mike Tirico, calling the game for ESPN, called it "one of the all-time bonehead plays."

Luckily for Jackson and the Eagles, none of the Cowboys players pounced on what was a live, loose ball on the field, so the officials gave the Eagles possession at the 2. They eventually scored the touchdown to go ahead 27–21, but lost the game to the Cowboys, 41–37.

When Dolphins kicker Garo Yepremian's field goal attempt was blocked late during the fourth quarter of Super Bowl VII in 1973, he was able to recover the ball. But instead of just falling on it—it was said he (being 5-foot-8 and 175 pounds) feared injury if the other players piled up on top of him—he attempted to throw it! Hardly a quarterback (he'd grown up as a soccer player in Cyprus) and with a defender in his face, the ball slipped right out of Yepremian's panicking hand, bounced off his arm, and went straight into the air.

With the ball hovering, Yepremian resorted to an attempt to swat the ball out of bounds, but instead tipped it right into the hands of Washington's Mike Bass, who returned the wayward kick for a touchdown.

It wound up being the only points Washington scored in the game, as Miami won, 14–7, to preserve its perfect season . . . even if Yepremian's style score was way less than a 10.

No one was able to tackle Daniel Jones . . . except for the Turf Monster!

In a 2020 game against the Eagles, the Giants quarterback took a designed run off the left side of the offensive line, cut up the field, and seemed destined to score on an incredible 88-yard dash. With no one in front of him, Jones blazed down the field at what would later be calculated as a mind-spinning 21.23 miles per hour. But around 20 yards away from the goal line things started to get away from Jones—mainly, his legs.

He lost his balance, tried to regain it, then stumbled to the ground eight yards shy of the end zone. That gave Eagles defenders a chance to catch up and touch him down for what would become an 80-yard run . . . and not a touchdown.

While Jones's teammates tried (mostly unsuccessfully) to hide their laughter, other NFL players watching the prime-time game weighed in on social media.

"He tripped the same way people do in scary movies when they running from the villain/bad guy," Bills wide receiver Stefon Diggs posted.

Wrote Patrick Mahomes: "I mean I can't even say anything because I would never be able to run that far either."

"I tried to run faster than I was running, and I got caught up," Jones told reporters after the game. "We finished the drive and scored a touchdown. That was a relief."

The Giants wound up losing the game, though, and Jones was saddled with a lowlight-reel play that will stick with him throughout his career.

Eugene Robinson received the prestigious Bart Starr Award from Athletes in Action the day before Super Bowl XXXIII in Miami for his "high moral character" and exemplifying "outstanding character and leadership in the home, on the field and in the community."

He found a strange way to celebrate.

That very night, the Falcons' veteran safety—who was playing in the championship game the following day—left his wife in the team hotel room, hit the town on his own, and tried to solicit a prostitute . . . only to find out she was an undercover cop.

Robinson was released in time to play in the big game, but not having gotten much sleep he was visibly sluggish and was burned by Rod Smith on an 80-yard touchdown that put the Broncos ahead, 17–3, in the second quarter. The Falcons lost the game, 34–19.

Oh, and Robinson wound up returning the Bart Starr Award.

Fifteen minutes wound up being not quite long enough for the Minnesota Vikings to make their first-round selection in the 2003 draft. They had the seventh overall selection and while negotiating potential trades with several teams for that spot—and had apparently agreed on a deal with the Ravens—their allotted time expired.

Because the trade was never finalized by the league before the team's time ran out, the official record showed that the Vikings simply passed on the pick. The rules allowed them to jump back in and make their selection at any point.

Before the Vikings could recombobulate, though, the Jaguars quickly pounced and made the seventh pick, quarterback Byron Leftwich. Then the Panthers jumped up and selected tackle Jordan Gross. Finally, the Vikings made what turned out to be the ninth overall selection and chose Kevin Williams. It was an embarrassing adventure for a franchise that had struggled with loose management for several years, but at least Williams wound up being a six-time Pro Bowler, five-time All-Pro, and a member of the HOF All-2000s team. Sometimes I guess it's better to be tardy then on time.

Dwayne Rudd definitely wasn't using his head in a game against the Chiefs in 2002. Nor was he using his helmet.

Thinking he had sacked Kansas City quarterback Trent Green on the final play to seal a win for Cleveland, Rudd grabbed his helmet through the ear holes, ripped it off his head, and beat his chest in celebration. Problem was, the game wasn't over.

Unbeknownst to Rudd, who had his back to the play, Green had flipped the ball to offensive tackle John Tait, who managed to run all the way to the Cleveland 25-yard line. Rudd was flagged for unsportsmanlike conduct (games cannot end on a defensive penalty) and the ball was moved halfway to the goal line to enforce the penalty, allowing Chiefs kicker Morten Anderson an opportunity to kick a 30-yard field goal with 0:00 showing on the clock. The kick was good, and the Chiefs won, 40–39.

Not only did Rudd's premature celebration cost the Browns a victory (and potentially their first double-digit-win season since 1994, before the team moved to Baltimore), it cost him a $5,000 fine from the league.

The Titans' 2013 season began with one of the silliest goofs in franchise history.

Tennessee returner Darius Reynaud was back to return the opening kickoff from the Pittsburgh Steelers. The ball bounced at the 5-yard-line and rolled back to Reynaud, who had jogged to the front of the end zone to retrieve it. Rather than attempt a return,

Reynaud opted to scoop up the ball and down it for a touchback. There was just one problem: Reynaud wasn't in the end zone when he picked up the ball.

Because he fielded the ball with one foot over the goal line, Reynaud downed himself into a safety. What should have been 1st-and-10 at the 20 turned into a 2–0 deficit and a free kick that gave the ball back to Pittsburgh.

Lucky for Reynaud, the Titans wound up winning the game, 16–9.

Aaron Brooks was inducted into the New Orleans Saints Hall of Fame in 2014, but ten years before that he was more likely to have landed in the Hall of Shame.

In a 2004 game against the Chargers, the quarterback tried to avoid a sack and, instead of throwing a forward pass, was spun around and wound up throwing the ball backwards. Running back Deuce McCallister eventually recovered the live lateral for a 25-yard loss and the Saints lost the game (to their future Super Bowl–winning quarterback Drew Brees), 43–17.

A year later, there was a glitch in some European versions of the *Madden NFL* video video game. Apparently, if you were playing in superstar mode and not controlling the quarterback, any pass thrown would wind up traveling backward. It became known as the "Aaron Brooks Glitch."

In a 2009 game against the Giants, Washington unveiled one of the most ill-conceived plays of all time: The Swinging Gate.

With his team down, 24–0, and just two seconds left in the first half, head coach Jim Zorn decided that, instead of attempting a field goal, he would dial up this beauty which, after lining up for a kick, had the entire offensive line shift all the way to the left sideline. That left just the snapper (tight end Todd Yoder), holder (punter Hunter Smith), and kicker (Graham Gano) in the middle of the field.

Once the ball was snapped to Smith—remember he is a punter, not a quarterback—there was no one to protect Smith and, to no one's surprise, he was immediately swarmed. In desperation, he chucked the ball about as high and far as he could. But there weren't any teammates near where the football came down, it was intercepted, and very nearly returned for a touchdown.

Finishing the season with a 4–12 record, Washington decided to relieve Zorn of his coaching duties. At least he didn't leave any unused pages in the playbook.

There were plenty of low points during the forgettable 2008 season when the Lions went 0–16, but the lowest had to have come when quarterback Dan Orlovsky, making his first start of the season, inadvertently ran out of bounds in the back of the end zone for a self-inflicted safety.

To make matters worse, Orlovsky seemed oblivious to the fact that he had ended the play. Even though the referee was signaling for the safety and Vikings defender Jared Allen, in pursuit, was laughing at the misguided scramble, Orlovsky kept running and looking downfield for a target to throw to.

The Vikings won that game, 12–10, the two-point difference coming on the ill-fated play.

Orlovsky wound up playing 13 years in the league, mostly as a backup, and has carved out a much more successful second career as an analyst for ESPN. But he is still haunted by that one play in which he lost track of where he was and unwittingly ran through the white out-of-bounds paint. He said he is confronted by the play "several times every day" on social media.

THE SULTAN OF SLIP-UPS

In the span of 10 months, Cowboys defensive lineman Leon Lett found himself in the middle of two of the most embarrassing, lame-brained plays in NFL history.

First, in Super Bowl XXVII against the Bills, Lett recovered a fumble on the Dallas 35-yard line late in a lopsided game, and ran it back toward the end zone. When he reached the 10-yard line, Lett slowed and held the ball out as he approached the goal line. However, in his preemptive celebration, he did not see Bills wide receiver Don Beebe chasing him down from behind. Beebe knocked the ball out of Lett's outstretched hand just before he crossed the goal line, which sent the ball through the end zone, resulting in a touchback. The Cowboys won the championship easily and didn't

(Continued on next page)

need those points, but they would have set the record for most points ever in a Super Bowl had Lett scored the touchdown.

The next season, in a Thanksgiving Day game against the Dolphins, his miscue cost the Cowboys a game. Dallas led, 14–13, with 15 seconds left in the game and Miami was attempting a 41-yard game-winning field goal. The kick was blocked by Lett's teammate, Jimmie Jones, and the ball came to rest several yards away. While most of the Cowboys began celebrating, knowing that they would get possession and the win once the play was whistled dead, Lett attempted to recover the ball. He slipped in the snow and sleet as he went down, however, and knocked the ball forward. In the resulting chase for possession, the Dolphins recovered it. That allowed them to attempt another game-winning kick, and this time it was good for a 16–14 Miami victory.

Even that gaffe wound up as a footnote rather than a dagger as the Cowboys never lost again the rest of the season and won Super Bowl XXVIII two months later.

One-Liners, Part I

Football players deliver plenty of touchdowns, big hits, and action every Sunday . . . and Monday . . . and Thursday . . . and sometimes Saturday (or future days that haven't yet been invented). But they also deliver some of the funniest lines of any athlete. Here are more than a few that have had teammates and fans chuckling through the years.

"I feel like I'm the best, but you're not going to get me to say that."
—Hall of Fame receiver Jerry Rice

"'Til I was thirteen, I thought my name was 'Shut Up.'"
—Hall of Fame quarterback Joe Namath

"I have two weapons: My arm, my legs, and my brain."
—Falcons quarterback Michael Vick

"Football is easy if you are crazy as hell."
—Raiders running back Bo Jackson

"You have to play this game like somebody just hit your mother with a two-by-four."
—Raiders defensive lineman Dan Birdwell

"Pro football is like nuclear warfare. There are no winners, only survivors."
—Hall of Famer Frank Gifford

"Most football players are temperamental. That's 90 percent temper and 10 percent mental."
—Bears safety Doug Plank

"If you're mad at your kid, you can either raise him to be a nose tackle or send him out to play on the freeway. It's about the same."
—defensive lineman Bob Golic

"I like to believe that my best hits border on felonious assault."
—Raiders safety Jack Tatum

"I love me some me!"
—Wide receiver Terrell Owens basking in the glow of, well, himself, on the sideline during a 49ers game against the Falcons. It was one of the early signs of Owens's large ego, but it certainly wasn't the last, as he'd go on to repeat the line at various points and with various teams as a sort of catchphrase throughout his career.

"I never graduated from Iowa, but I was only there for two terms—Truman's and Eisenhower's."
—Hall of Famer Alex Karras

"Let's face it, you have to have a slightly recessive gene that has a little something to do with the brain to go out on the football field and beat your head against other human beings on a daily basis."
—NFL defensive lineman Tim Green

"I'm a firm believer that all sports will eventually be global. Someday, we may have a quarterback from China named Yao Fling."
—former NFL Commissioner Paul Tagliabue

"I'm a light eater. As soon as it's light, I start to eat."
—Hall of Fame lineman Art Donovan

"The only way to stop Jim Brown was to give him a movie contract."
—Giants defensive back Carl "Spider" Lockhart on the Hall of Famer who put his football career on hold to pursue acting

"Rapport? You mean, like, 'You'll run as fast as you can, and I'll throw it as far as I can?'"
—NFL quarterback Jeff Kemp on the simplicity of building chemistry with his receivers

"You have to be mean to be a football player. Some of the best players don't know how to be mean, and that's why they can't get their team to the next level. I'm super mean on the field. If my mom was out there, I'd run over her."
—NFL defensive lineman Michael Bennett

"I'm 6-foot-7, a big black guy running down the middle of the field. I wear white gloves so [quarterback Jay Cutler] can see the white gloves when I wave them like Mickey Mouse."
—Bears tight end Martellus Bennett

Patriots linebacker Rob Ninkovich had no idea how to respond after he tackled Colts quarterback Andrew Luck, and Luck congratulated him on a nice hit. "Thanks for, uh, accepting the hit," Ninkovich responded.

Bears defensive lineman Jared Allen often marveled at how folks reacted to his mullet haircut. "You know, football's the same way. 'Hey, check out this dude with a mullet. Oh, wait, he just body slammed me, and my quarterback is on the ground.' See? It's just that people are caught off guard."

Ravens wide receiver Steve Smith Sr. was once asked about the excitement of playing in prime-time nationally televised games. "Family members get to see you play," he said. "Ex-girlfriends that wished they wouldn't have dumped you, they're questioning themselves right now. So, it's fun."

"You have to be stupid, and that's working out well for me."
—Pro Bowl defensive end Al "Bubba" Baker, on what it takes to play in the NFL

"Physically, he's a world-beater. Mentally, he's an eggbeater."
—Michigan center Matt Elliott on Ohio State defender Alonzo Spellman

POETRY BY PRIME

Deion "Prime Time" Sanders, one of the best cornerbacks in NFL history, began his pro career with the Falcons and after five seasons signed with the 49ers. After his one year in San Francisco was over and was a free agent once again, Sanders was asked if there was a chance he might return to Atlanta.

"You don't go from a Yugo to a Benz and back to a Yugo," he said.

In Sanders-speak, that was a no.

Here are a few other memorable lines from one of the more verbose and colorful players in football history:

When he was selected by the Falcons in the draft, he said of an upcoming deal: "There's gonna be a lot of zeroes in that contract. You're gonna think it's alphabet soup or something, all those zeroes in there."

(Continued on next page)

On his priorities when it came to his side career as a major-league baseball player: "I'm married to football. Baseball is my girlfriend."

On returning a punt for a touchdown: "I felt like a deer with a hundred hunters after me."

On his ability to take away large parts of the field defensively: "Water covers two-thirds of the Earth. I cover the rest."

"Confidence is my natural odor."

"If you look good, you feel good. If you feel good, you play good. If you play good, they pay good."

"I never wear the same shoes twice."

"People say there's no 'I' in team. Well, there's not. But there's an 'I' in win."

And when he and his Cowboys teammates were mocked for traveling in limos before Super Bowl XXX against the Steelers, Sanders quipped: "Sure we're in limos. We're stars. How else is a star supposed to travel?"

Coachspeak, Part I

John McKay had the unenviable job of coaching the expansion Tampa Bay Buccaneers which went winless in their first season, 1976, and didn't notch a victory until Week 13 of their second season after starting out 0–26. The comically bad football at least spurred some humorous lines and quips from McKay during his press conferences and other appearances. McKay's career record in the NFL was a measly 44–88–1, but, in spite of that (or perhaps because of it), he became the undisputed champion of coaching one-liners. Among them:

He assessed his team's debut performance in its preseason opener as such: "We didn't tackle well today but we made up for it by not blocking."

He once compared coaching an expansion team to a religious experience: "You do a lot of praying, but most of the time the answer is 'no.'"

"Emotion is highly overrated in football," he said. "My wife Corky is emotional as hell but can't play football worth a damn."

During the long losing streak, he noted how close the Bucs were to being a playoff team. "Three or four plane crashes and we're in."

"We can't stop a pass or a run," he said of his defense. "Otherwise, we're in great shape."

On the play of Joe Namath in the Jets' 34–0 victory over Tampa Bay, he said: "Namath is still Namath, but I must say that our guys were nice to him. I noticed when they knocked him down, they helped him to his feet. That was gentlemanly. I thought one stood around long enough to get his autograph."

He recalled a 42–0 loss on a very cold day in Pittsburgh: "We had no players and the ones we did have wanted to stay at the hotel by the fire. I was ticked because that's where I wanted to stand."

Of that same lopsided game, he said: "There were times I felt like leaving the stadium and hitchhiking home."

When placekicker Pete Rajecki claimed he had a bad camp with the Buccaneers because McKay made him nervous, he said: "I don't think he's got much of a future here, because I plan on going to all the games."

After another tough loss McKay was asked what he thought of his team's execution. His reply: "I'm all for it."

McKay made it clear which city was his least favorite to play in. "If a contest had ninety-seven prizes, the ninety-eighth would be a trip to Green Bay."

Of course, the Bucs didn't have much success on the road in any city. "Well, we've determined that we can't win at home and we can't win on the road. What we need is a neutral site."

Once that first miserable season was over he addressed any of the players who planned on remaining in Tampa during the offseason. "Stop by my office tomorrow and pick up some fake noses and mustaches so no one recognizes your sorry asses."

McKay certainly wasn't the only football coach known to come up with a few zingers and belly laughers. Here are a few other gems that have come from football's *supposed* leaders of men:

"Football isn't a contact sport. It's a collision sport. Dancing is a contact sport."
—Hall of Fame coach Vince Lombardi

"Football is, after all, a wonderful way to get your aggressions out without going to jail for it."
—Ohio State head coach Woody Hayes

"Luck means a lot in football. Not having a quarterback is bad luck."
—Hall of Fame coach Don Shula

"Gentlemen, it is better to have died a small boy than to fumble this football."
—college football coach John Heisman, namesake of the trophy and author of *Principles of Football*

"The purpose of the center during the snap is to get the ball to the quarterback, and if that doesn't happen it usually results in a fumble."
—Hall of Fame coach John Madden

"Most of my clichés aren't original."
—Rams head coach Chuck Knox

"We couldn't do diddly poo offensively."
—Saints coach Jim Mora, on his team's inability to score

"If I drop dead tomorrow, at least I'll know I died in good health."
—Oilers head coach Bum Phillips

"It's hard to believe the score started at 0–0."
—Dennis Green, after his Northwestern team lost to Iowa, 64–0

"We're not attempting to circumcise the rules." —Steelers head coach Bill Cowher

"We can't run. We can't pass. We can't stop the run. We can't stop the pass. We can't kick. Other than that, we're just not a very good football team right now."
—Bengals head coach Bruce Coslet

PETERSON'S PARODIES

If anyone comes close to John McKay's penchant for funny phrases it would have to be former Oilers head coach Bill Peterson, who was known for his many malaprops when it came to directing his players on and off the field.

One time he instructed them to "line up alphabetically by height."

On another instance, he barked: "You guys pair up in groups of three, then line up in a circle."

He urged his players to recall the immortal words of Patrick Henry ("Give me liberty or give me death!") before botching the line and insisting it was: "Kill me or let me live!"

"Men, I want you just thinking of one word all season," Peterson once said. "One word and one word only: Super Bowl."

Appealing to a higher authority prior to a game he once asked his captains to "lead us in a few words of silent prayer."

And just in case anyone had other ideas of who was in charge, Peterson once barked: "I'm the football coach around here, and don't you remember it!"

Jokey Jokes, Part II

Known for his brute strength during his playing career, Bob Biceps retired and lived the rest of his life running a service station in a small town. A reporter came along looking to interview the former football star and began asking questions around town.

"Oh sure, I know Bob Biceps," one of the locals said. "Once someone gets their gas from Bob, they never go anyplace else."

"Is the service that good?" the reporter asked.

The local thought about it. "Come to think of it, no, not really," he said.

"Does he have the best prices?"

"Actually he usually runs about five to ten cents more expensive than everybody else in town."

"Well then, the gas must be better?"

"No," the local said, "it's just the same regular gas as all the other stations."

"Then why does everyone keep coming back to Bob Biceps's gas station?" the reporter asked.

"Because," the local said, "when Bob puts your gas cap on, nobody else but him can get it off again."

What football game do cats love to watch the most? The Goldfish Bowl.

Which football team serves the smallest drinks at its concession stand? The Mini-soda Vikings.

Why wasn't the sausage getting any playing time? Because it was the wurst on the team.

What do you call a big monkey who scores the winning touchdown? A chimp-ion.

What is a mean football coach's favorite color? Yeller.

Why did the skeleton retire from football? His heart wasn't in it.

What ocean creature is best at playing defense? The octopus, because it has ten tackles.

What deadly animal is surprisingly good at football? A score-pion.

Why did the frog head to the equipment room? To get fitted for his lily pads.

Why did the receiver quit? Opportunities kept slipping right through his fingers.

Why did the members of the high school Mathletes attend the football game? To square root for the home team.

Which insect should you never pick for your football team? A fumble bee.

Sammy Simpleton made a lot of money playing football and owned four large estates. One day his real estate broker came to him with another one that he could buy. Sam thought about it for a moment.

"OK," he said, "but first I have to sell one of the other properties."

"Why?" asked the realtor.

"Because," Sammy said, "I don't want to get a five-yard penalty."

Classic Pranks

Even the greatest quarterback of all time couldn't evade one of football's most time-honored traditions: the rookie prank.

When Tom Brady was in his first season with the Patriots in 2000, Drew Bledsoe was still the team's starter and undisputed leader.

"He was like an eager little puppy," Bledsoe said of Brady. "From the minute he got there, he was always super positive and upbeat . . . sometimes annoyingly so."

Bledsoe and other veteran teammates decided he would be ripe for a prank.

"So the FBI, if they think there is going to be a bank robbery, they have this special dye that they put on the money. And you can't see it at all until it gets slightly wet. So just a little perspiration on your hands and then it's permanent. So we were able to lay our hands on some of this FBI stuff and we filled Tommy's socks full of it. He goes out to practice. His feet sweat. He comes back in and his feet are bright purple . . . for weeks."

That certainly wasn't the only time Brady was the target of a prank from teammates. Even later in his career after he'd won multiple Super Bowls, he was still on the receiving end of them. In 2005, *GQ* magazine profiled him and ran some sultry photos of him wearing cowboy gear and frolicking with golden retrievers. There was even one that had Brady in a sleeveless white shirt and thick leather gloves while holding a goat.

"It takes a lot of man to hold a lamb," wide receiver Deion Branch laughed when asked what he thought of the spread.

Offensive linemen Matt Light and Dan Koppen decided to have fun at Brady's expense by taping those pictures to the backs of their jerseys so that Brady would see them when he lined up to take snaps at practice. It didn't take long, though, for Brady to realize what was happening, chase down the linemen, and rip the photos from their backs.

"I got it bad today, probably the worst I've ever gotten," Brady said. "I think I'm going to have to deal with it for the next few days, but I guess I deserve it."

In 2005, rookie quarterback Kyle Orton of the Bears was approached by teammate Olin Kreutz and asked to autograph a helmet for a family member who was a huge fan. Of course, Orton obliged. Little did he know, however, that there was no family member. The helmet Orton signed was actually his own and, later that day, when the team went out to practice, Orton had to endure the workout in a helmet with his own signature on it.

Chris Colmer was a rookie offensive lineman with the Bucs in 2005, when Mike Alstott asked him to bring some Gatorades for him and a few other veterans. Colmer thought it would be funny to instead bring Alstott a map of where the Gatorades were stored rather than the Gatorades themselves. Rookie mistake. A few days later Alstott had the tires removed from Colmer's car in the players' lot, putting it up on blocks, and gave Colmer a map of where to find the missing wheels.

Eli Manning may have come across as one of the more mild-mannered players during his 16-year career, but behind the scenes he had a reputation for being a voracious practical joker.

"I would change some peoples' phones and change their wives' number with Coach [Tom] Coughlin's number so when they thought they were texting their wife, they were texting Coach Coughlin," Manning said. "I'm sure he got some interesting texts over that. I don't know if I ever got called guilty on that or if they knew it was me but that was an early favorite that we had some laughs with."

Manning also became very adept at swiping the cellphones of teammates and, before it was even noticed missing, switching the default language from English to Chinese. The poor victim, unable to decipher the symbols on the screen, would not be able to navigate through the menus to return the language to English.

Odell Beckham Jr. recalled another of Manning's go-to pranks:

"He'd be around the rookies after practice, and he'd start rubbing his cheek. He'd make this face like he was in pain, and he'd tell them he had a toothache. He'd press down on his cheek and move his jaw like he was in serious pain. He'd be like 'Oh, man, I just got my wisdom teeth pulled not long ago. Do you ever hurt like that in your mouth?' So he'd ask a guy if he still had his wisdom teeth. And, of course, the rookies would, like, open wide and try to show him. And he'd take his other hand and shove the pellets from the artificial turf in their mouths."

Ted Walsh, a former assistant equipment manager for the 49ers, told the following story to the *Los Angeles Times* in 2019 of an annual prank:

"Every year in New Orleans, the game day programs came out and they'd put one on everybody's chair. We'd have the locker room attendants in the visiting locker rooms come in and say, 'Hey, guys, there's been a mistake. One of the prizes that's been issued got mixed up in your programs. There's a page in there that if Rickey Jackson signed page 97 of your program, that person's getting a car.' We'd prearranged it and I had signed Rickey Jackson's name in the program on his picture. The one year we sat it on Jamie Williams's seat, the tight end. So the guy comes in and makes the announcement and you see all the guys looking in their programs. Jamie jumps up, turns around, and he's looking at it. Jerry [Rice's] locker is right next to him, and Jerry's playing it up.

"Jamie's like, 'Man, my family's here. I could give it to my mom, and then she could win the car.' We were watching the whole thing play out. He's trying to think about what he could do, how he could get this car. It was hilarious."

Before he was a Super Bowl–winning Hall of Fame coach, Tony Dungy was just a rookie with the Steelers. And that made him the target of pranks.

"In October I remember Franco [Harris] coming up to me and telling me that for Thanksgiving all the rookies got a turkey, but that he knew I probably didn't know how to cook one, so would I mind giving mine to him. I said, 'sure.' About six weeks later, Mel

Blount came up to me and asked if I could give my turkey to him, saying that his wife would cook it and invite all the defensive backs over to eat it. I told him I liked that idea, but I had already promised my turkey to Franco. Mel told me Franco was just being selfish and he did that every year. So I asked Franco if he would mind me giving it to Mel and he said sure, and that he'd just get one from one of the rookie offensive linemen.

"Well, the night before Thanksgiving, Mel told me that Jim Boston had my turkey and that I should go get it from him. So I went to his office and he said I should get it from Dan Rooney. So I went to him and he told me he'd just given the last one to Coach [Chuck] Noll, that he felt really bad and it wasn't like them to make this kind of a mistake. He told me I should just go ask Chuck for it.

"I went back to Mel and told him there was no way I was going to ask Chuck Noll for his turkey! The whole room started laughing."

Turned out there were no free turkeys, and that the entire organization was involved in trying to get Dungy to ask the head coach for his bird.

"I knew other teams played jokes on their players," Dungy said, "I just didn't see this coming."

Disses

Every year there is a champion in football. And every year there is a handful of teams that can't get out of their own way, that have a long history of failure, whose fans have become jaded and hardened by defeat, and whose prospects never seem to improve.

Those teams may change but, luckily for us, the jokes hardly ever do.

Since we're printing this book in 2024, we'll present the following classic disses aimed at some of the NFL's current and long-suffering low-hanging fruit: the Jets, the Browns, the Cowboys, the Panthers, and the Bills. If, for some unforeseeable reason in the future, the fortunes of those teams should change, well, the good news is you are free to swap any other team in their place and still enjoy the jokes!

Why don't the Browns have a web address? Because they can't string together three W's.

What do you call fifty-three millionaires sitting around a television watching the Super Bowl? The Dallas Cowboys.

Why is the Panthers' home field filled with brown spots no matter how many times it gets resodded? Not even the grass will root for them.

What do you call a Jets player with a Super Bowl ring? A thief.

What do the Browns and opossums have in common? Both play dead at home and get killed on the road.

What does a Panthers fan do when his team wins the Super Bowl? He turns off his PlayStation.

What do the Browns have in common with Charlie Chaplin? All their best moments are in black and white.

Did you hear about the Bills kicker who tried to throw himself on the floor in a fit of disgust? He missed.

The Dallas Cowboys visited an orphanage. "It was sad to see their little faces with no hope whatsoever," said five-year-old Owen.

The Panthers are game changers. Every time their game is on TV, viewers change the channel.

How many Jets does it take to change a tire? One, unless it's a blowout, in which case they all show up.

The Ohio state troopers are getting serious about enforcing the speeding laws. If they catch you, for the first offense, they give you two Browns tickets. If you get stopped a second time, they make you use them.

Two parents in Dallas were arrested by child services for putting their toddler in a Cowboys jersey. It was deemed a choking hazard.

What's the difference between an onion and a Jets jersey? No one cries when you cut up a Jets jersey.

The dumbest burglar in the world? The one who breaks into the Bills' trophy room.

Did you hear how the Panthers finally won? The other team didn't show up and it only took the Panthers five plays to score the game-winning touchdown.

Crime is getting really bad. I had two Jets tickets in my car and someone smashed the passenger window and left four more of them.

A guy walks into a bar with his dog. The bartender points to a sign that says, "No Pets Allowed."

"Please," the guy says, "this is a very special dog. He does back-flips every time the Jets kick a field goal."

The bartender seems skeptical but humors the man and turns the game on the television. Pretty soon the Jets kick a field goal and the dog does several backflips.

"That is pretty amazing!" the bartender says. "What does the dog do when the Jets score a touchdown?"

"How should I know?" the guy says. "I've only had the dog five years."

Snow White was walking through the woods with her friends when, all of a sudden, the seven of them fell into a deep dark ravine. Snow White ran to the edge and yelled down to see if they were still alive. From the depths of the gorge came a lone voice. "The Panthers are legitimate Super Bowl contenders!" one of them called out.

"Oh, thank goodness!" Snow White shouted. "At least Dopey survived."

On the first day of school, the second-grade teacher tells her class that she is a Bills fan and asks her students to raise their hands if they are as well. Not wanting to get on her bad side, most of them raised their hands. In the back row, though, one little girl sat with her arms folded.

"Why didn't you raise your hand?" the teacher asked.

"Because I'm a Patriots fan," the girl said.

"And why are you a Patriots fan?" the teacher asked.

"Well, my mom is a Patriots fan and my dad is a Patriots fan so I am a Patriots fan, too," she said.

The teacher was annoyed.

"That's no reason to root for a team," the teacher said. "You don't have to be just like your parents all of the time. What if your mom was an idiot and your dad was a moron, what would you be then?"

The little girl thought about it.

"Then," she said, "I'd probably be a Bills fan."

Four Bills fans were complaining about their team.

"I blame the general manager," the first one said. "We'd be a great team if he signed and drafted better players."

"I blame the coach," the second one said. "He never calls the right play at the right time."

"I blame the players," the third one said. "If they gave better effort they'd score more touchdowns."

"I blame my parents," the fourth one said.

"Your parents?" the others asked. "What did they do?"

"If I'd been born in New England instead of Buffalo," he said, "I'd have won six championships by now!"

Media Mayhem

Traditionally, reporters don't like to become part of the story they are covering. That's less true now with some so-called journalists looking to improve their brand recognition by leaning into outrageous hot takes and flaunting cozy relationships that often cross the long-established lines of professional standards, but for the most part the majority of those covering the NFL still adhere to a proper distancing and perspective.

Sometimes, though, they can't help but become characters in the narrative they are telling.

Here are a few times when a reporter was swallowed up by a story they were trying to cover:

Kyle Shanahan, then the offensive coordinator for the Falcons who was about to become head coach of the 49ers, spent an hour on the hot seat answering questions during Media Night at Super Bowl LI in Houston. It turned out to be the easiest part of his evening. The most difficult? When he got up from his chair and realized that his backpack, which contained the Atlanta game plan for the upcoming contest against the Patriots, almost fifty tickets for friends and family to attend the game, and a few thousand dollars in cash, had disappeared. “I was very panicked,” Shanahan would later say. “The whole team left me. The Patriots came in and I was walking around there looking for my backpack frantically, running into more media people and still having to do interviews past my deal. I was trying not to come off as a jerk blowing them off, but I was certainly stressed trying to find my backpack.” After scouring the area looking for the lost knapsack and with speculation running rampant—was this one of Bill Belichick’s dirty tricks?—it was eventually discovered that sportswriter Art Spander had mistakenly grabbed Shanahan’s bag while intending to reach for his own. Spander was tracked down and returned the bag, and its valuable contents, to Shanahan. “I forgave him fast,” Shanahan said, “but I was stressed for a while.”

During a media session before Super Bowl XV, Raiders quarterback Jim Plunkett was trying to tell reporters about his hard-luck beginnings. Sportswriter Bus Saidt still needed some clarification. “I’m having trouble keeping this straight,” he asked. “Is it blind mother, dead father? Or blind father, dead mother?” Both of Plunkett’s parents were blind, and his father was dead. The quarterback paused before setting the record straight in front of a group of stunned onlookers.

One of the most infamous—and cringiest—questions in Super Bowl history was never quite asked the way it was portrayed, but has become such a part of NFL lore that it might as well have been. When Doug Williams became the first Black quarterback to start a Super Bowl in January 1988, he faced his fair share of questions about setting history. The most remembered one: "Doug, how long havc you been a Black quarterback?" The question reporter Butch John *actually* asked was: "Doug, it's obvious you've been a Black quarterback all your life. When did it start to matter?" John was trying to be funny and most of those who were around him—including Williams—got the joke from the first part of the question. Unfortunately, the inaccurately paraphrased version took on a life of its own, and is the one that still gets all the attention.

Not all media questions are inadvertently funny. The Super Bowl draws all kinds of outlets, including those that don't normally cover football, as well as thosc who specialize in satire and farce. So it was that in 2000 a reporter from Comedy Central's *The Daily Show* managed to get close enough to Titans defensive lineman Jevon Kearse and ask about his jewelry: "What's the significance of the cross?"

Jewelry was part of a question for Broncos running back Bobby Humphrey in 1990, when he was asked why he takes the huge sparkly earrings that he was wearing for Media Day out for the games. He said it was because he didn't want the diamonds "to be pushed through my ear to the middle of my brain."

Someone asked Ravens tight end Dennis Pitta before Super Bowl XLVII, "On a scale of 1 to 10, how ticklish are you?" Pitta's answer: "I'm probably a five or six. You know, moderately ticklish. Good question."

ASK AND YE SHALL *NOT* RECEIVE

Media Day for Super Bowl XXXIV was legendary for some off-the-wall questions, and may have produced the greatest ratio of guffaws and grimaces to queries in Super Bowl history. Among the conversations that took place between players and reporters on that one single day:

A question for St. Louis defensive lineman Jay Williams regarding his team's nickname: "Is Ram a noun or a verb?"

Titans defensive tackle Joe Salave'a was asked: "What's your relationship with the football?" Salave'a's answer: "I'd say it's strictly platonic."

Rams offensive tackle Orlando Pace was asked: "After the game, in the shower, what's your favorite bar of soap?"

Rams receiver Isaac Bruce had been in a car accident during that 1999 season, and was talking to reporters about the incident. "When I flipped in my car, I called on the name of Jesus," he said. "That's the name that I know saves me. And when I did that, I knew everything would be fine." One reporter, wanting to use the proper quote, asked for clarification. "So, did you say 'Jesus, Jesus, Jesus?' Or just 'Jesus?'" Bruce's response: "It was one Jesus."

Then there was this one for Rams quarterback Kurt Warner: "Kurt, two questions: Do you believe in voodoo? And can I have a lock of your hair?" Warner's simple one-word response that seemed to answer both of those topics: "No."

The best part about Media Day for many folks, of course, is when players have a chance to stick it to reporters. That was certainly the case with Seahawks running back Marshawn Lynch, who showed up to the event as close to incognito as he could get, with a hood pulled up on his head and sunglasses on. He didn't field any questions and delivered a terse statement: "I'm just 'bout that action, Boss."

A year later the Seahawks were back in the Super Bowl and Lynch was threatened with a $500,000 fine if he failed to show up for the required availability. He did. Grudgingly.

Over the course of four minutes and fifty-one seconds Lynch was asked twenty-nine questions. To each of them he gave the same general answer, with some variety in cadence and wording: "I'm just here so I won't get fined."

It worked. He wasn't.

It was another running back, though, who delivered perhaps the best knockout punch any player has come up with in response to the long, tedious dance with the media. In 1994, when Bills running back Thurman Thomas was getting ready to play in his fourth straight Super Bowl after losing the previous three, someone asked him how he gets himself psyched up for big games. He rolled his eyes.

"I read the newspaper," he said, "and look at the stupid questions you all ask."

QUESTIONABLE QUESTIONS

Here are a few of the all-time strangest, funniest, and oddest (purposefully or not, you be the judge) questions ever asked during Super Bowl Media Days, most of which don't even need an answer to provide a punchline:

"What are you going to wear in the game on Sunday?"

"Are you going to listen to Stevie Wonder perform at halftime?"

(Continued on next page)

"What size panties do you think you'd wear?"

This one was asked of Steelers linebacker Kevin Greene, whose long blond locks were a source of conversation: "How long does it take you to wash your hair?"

"Do you believe you can win?"

"Can I have your pants?"

Super Bowl XXVII was played at the Rose Bowl, but Media Day was at Dodgers Stadium, which prompted this query for Troy Aikman of the Cowboys: "Does it seem a little strange answering football questions in a baseball stadium?"

"Would you like to see the AFC win the Super Bowl?"

"What are the words to the *SportsCenter* theme song?"

"Do you ever skip to the end of the playbook and read the last page as a spoiler?"

"Is this a must-win game?"

And finally . . .

"So, why do they call you Boomer?"

That certainly seemed like a fair enough question for Bengals quarterback Boomer Esiason before Super Bowl XXIII. Too bad it was asked of 49ers quarterback Joe Montana instead!

Jokey Jokes, Part III

Nate Noble, the star running back, hurt his hamstring and couldn't go back onto the field. The team doctor took one look at him, pulled out a heating pad, placed it on Nate's leg, and told him to count slowly to 120. Just as he reached the final number, Nate sprung up from the sideline and raced back on the field to help win the game.

"I've never seen anything like that miracle cure of yours," the appreciative coach said to the doctor afterward. "What do you call it?"

Said the doctor: "The two-minute warming."

A new rule proposed by the NFL will prohibit players from keeping chickens as pets. They will be regarded as personal fowls.

Which football player smells the best? The scenter.

How do you sack the Dolphins' quarterback? With fishing tackle.

How did Ebenezer Scrooge score the game-winning touchdown? The Ghost of Christmas Passed.

What do football players eat at picnics? Hut-dogs.

What's a football player's favorite part of a joke? The punt-line.

What position did the pig play on the farm's football team? Swinebacker.

What is a die-hard fan's favorite drink? Root beer.

What animal would make the best referee? A canary, because it knows how to whistle.

Why did the football player wear armor instead of his usual pads? He was told it was a knight game.

What do you call a lineman's kid? A chip off the old blocker.

What happened when the football players asked to have onions on their burgers instead of pickles? They were flagged for an illegal substitution.

Billy Bumbles dropped four passes, missed five blocks, fumbled a handoff, and was called for three penalties before he hurt his leg and was taken to the training room. Eventually he came back to the sideline with the bad news.

"Sorry, Coach," Billy groaned, "but the doctor said I can't play football."

"Billy," Coach said, "we didn't need a doctor to figure that out."

Wife: "I want a divorce. He's too obsessed with football."

Therapist: "How long have you been married?"

Husband: "Five seasons."

Heads Or Tails?

NFL games can sometimes be impacted by the toss of a coin—especially when it happens in overtime—but rarely does the ceremonial pregame flip result in something as serious as a suspension. That was the case in Charlotte in December 2023, though, when Packers cornerback Jaire Alexander crashed one of the most banal parts of a Sunday contest, turning it into one of the oddest of all time.

Alexander appointed himself a captain for the Packers and trotted out to meet with the officials without clearing it with head coach Matt LeFleur. He then called the toss (correctly!) and declared that the Packers wanted to start the game on defense. That's different than deferring, which many teams do in order to receive the kickoff at the start of the second half. Had Alexander's request been adhered to as stated, the Panthers would have received *both* of the game's two ordained kickoffs! Luckily for the Packers, referee Alex Kemp asked for clarification.

"They all looked at me like I was crazy," Alexander said after the game. "He was like 'Do you mean defer?' I was like 'I guess' . . . I was like, 'What are you all laughing at?'"

The Packers won the game, 33–30, but Alexander was suspended the following week for "conduct detrimental to the team" during that event. The blunder not only cost him a chance to help the Packers on the field, but $60,000 in lost salary.

Alexander isn't the only one to make a mistake between "defending" and "deferring." In 2019, Cowboys quarterback Dak Prescott won the coin toss in a game against the Rams. He told referee Walt Anderson that Dallas wanted "defense." Then he pointed in the direction he wanted the Cowboys to head and said: "Kicking that way." Then, finally, after a quizzical look from Anderson, Prescott tried to clarify and said: "We defer to the second half." But it was too late. Anderson announced that he was sticking with Prescott's initial two requests. The entire first half was played with the expectation that the Cowboys would kick off to start the second half. However, officials reviewed the video (and audio) at halftime and reversed the decision.

Just about everything leading up to the action in a Super Bowl is ironed out ahead of time, but in 2014 the coin toss for Super Bowl XLVIII went completely off script. Joe Namath, who strolled out to the field wearing a long fur coat that summoned memories of his glory days with the Jets, was there to flip the coin. Terry McAuley handed it to Namath but, before McAuley could ask the visiting Seahawks if they wanted heads or tails, Namath tossed it in the air. Luckily, McAuley was able to snag it before it hit the turf ("That was a nice catch," Phil Simms told him). McAuley then asked Seattle for their decision (tails) before handing the coin back to Namath. "Now, Joe," McAuley said. "I always had a quick release," Namath said with an impish smile before the official and legitimate toss, which Seattle won. It was one of the more entertaining aspects of a game that quickly headed toward a lopsided 43–8 win for the Seahawks.

No one may have ever been as excited about a coin toss as Giants safety Jabrill Peppers in an overtime game against the Saints in 2021. Asked for his call to start the extra period, Peppers said: "Heads, baby, heads! I'm confident!" Before referee Greg Gautreaux was able to announce that the coin did in fact come up heads, Peppers screamed "Boom!" and then yelled, "We want that [blankety-blank], man!" The Giants did get it and scored to win the game on their first possession.

While Peppers's salty words may have been heard a little too clearly for some delicate tastes, coin tosses can run amok when players don't speak up, too. That was the case for a Thanksgiving game between the Steelers and Lions in 1998. With the contest heading into overtime, Steelers running back Jerome Bettis called "tails" while the coin was in the air (the NFL has since altered this procedure and now has visiting teams call it before the coin is actually tossed). Referee Phil Luckett misheard Bettis. "'Heads' is the call," Luckett said. "I said tails!" Bettis argued. "He said heads. It is tails," a mic'd-up Luckett said to the Lions, Steelers, and 78,139 in attendance at the Silverdome. Luckett later tried to explain to an irate Steelers sideline that he first heard Bettis call heads then switch to tails, but replays showed that was not the case. The Lions, who technically lost the toss, decided to receive. "I looked at Ray and was like, 'We'll take the ball,'" Lions captain Robert Porcher later recalled. "Jerome was like, 'Wait a minute! What's going on here?' [But] I just ran back to the sideline, and I couldn't believe it . . . We weren't going to correct it." The Lions received the overtime kickoff and kicked the game-winning field goal without the Steelers ever touching the ball.

Sometimes seeing is more difficult than hearing for the officials. In a 2003 game between the Patriots and Dolphins, the Patriots called "tails" for the overtime flip. Referee Gerry Austin tossed the coin in the air and the Patriots players began celebrating, believing it landed tails up. The only problem was that Austin saw it as "heads" and declared the Dolphins as the winners of the toss. He picked it up too quickly for anyone to be certain of what happened and there was confusion over which side of the coin had actually come up. Despite lengthy protests from the Patriots, Miami received the kickoff. No matter, though, as the Dolphins missed a field goal and the Patriots won on a Tom Brady touchdown pass.

Finally, one of the most confounding and confusing coin toss conversations of all time came at the start of a Jets game against the Jaguars in 2012. Jacksonville won the toss and elected to defer, so all the Jets had to do was say they wanted the ball. Instead, Jets captain Tim Tebow—a hero in Florida for his collegiate exploits but otherwise a nonparticipant in this game—indicated that the Jets wanted to go in a certain direction. "You want the ball?" referee Alberto Riveron asked, but Tebow said: "We'll defend this goal." There was an awkward pause. Tebow then covered all his bases and said: "Yeah, we want to defer." Riveron had to tell Tebow that the Jaguars had already deferred. "We want to defend this goal," Tebow said again, pointing to the far end zone. Patiently, Riveron explained the consequences of that choice. “That means they are going to get the ball twice,” he said. “No,” Tebow said. “We’ll take it.” Finally, the right answer! “So, you want the ball then,” an exhausted Riveron said with an audible sigh. “Good.”

GREEN BAY COIN BUNGLES

The Packers seem to find themselves in quite a few funny and strange coin toss moments.

In 2008, a December game against the Bears in Chicago went to overtime. Ryan Grant of the Packers called tails and referee Ron Winter sent the coin into the air, but it veered off to the left and bounced off the helmet of Bears captain Brian Urlacher. That resulted in a scurry to find the wayward coin before it was eventually spotted. It came up—what else?—heads. The Bears won the game on a field goal on their first possession, too.

(Continued on next page)

In January 2016, those same Packers were in another overtime game, this time a playoff game against the Cardinals. Referee Clete Blakeman gathered the captains at midfield and went over the implications of the toss before asking Packers quarterback Aaron Rodgers for a call. He called tails and it came up heads. Fairly simple, right? Wrong. Because this was the coin flip that didn't flip. It simply went up in the air and came down without any revolution or tumbling. Almost immediately the Packers objected and Blakeman called a rare do-over. "It didn't flip," Blakeman said from the field. "It didn't flip." Now it was the Cardinals who objected. But Blakeman tossed it again, this time with the necessary torque, and it came up heads just as before. The Cardinals received and scored a touchdown to win on the first drive of overtime.

Perhaps the greatest coin toss in Packers history, though, was in overtime of a playoff game at Lambeau Field against the Seahawks in 2004. Seattle won that toss and quarterback Matt Hasselbeck said, into the referee's open microphone so everyone in the stadium and everyone watching at home could hear, "We want the ball, and we're going to score." Well, Seattle got the ball, but Packers defender Al Harris intercepted a Hasselbeck pass on the sixth play of the Seahawks' second overtime possession and returned it 52 yards to give the Packers a 33–27 victory.

Insult to Injury

One of the most ridiculous injuries in NFL history happened in the Jaguars' locker room in 2003, when Pro Bowl punter Chris Hanson picked up an ax, swung it at an oak stump, and ended up slicing open his leg with a season-ending gash that left blood splattered on the carpet.

Before you ask, first-year coach Jack Del Rio had the double-edged ax that was painted in team colors and the old stump placed in the locker room to illustrate his "keep chopping wood" motivational slogan. Occasionally players would take the advice literally and swing the tool while taking chunks from the stump. When Hanson gave it a whirl, the blade either bounced off the stump or went through a piece of it (versions vary) and buried itself in Hanson's right leg.

"I'll find another slogan," was all Del Rio could say. "The message was understood. The thing was on its way out soon, but not soon enough. It was symbolic more than anything else."

Hanson was sewn up and wound up playing six more seasons in the NFL. The stump, on the other hand, was properly disposed of. But the ax? It was kept in the office of Mike Perkins, the director of football technology and facilities for the Jaguars, for many years. Perkins had purchased the ax and found the stump at Del Rio's request. It remains among the team artifacts.

"It's a part of Jaguars history, is it not?" Jeff Lageman, a Jaguars Hall of Famer, told ESPN of the ax. "It's a weird part, but it is a part of Jaguars history and Jaguars history should always be kept."

Oddly enough, that wasn't Hanson's only injury sustained under . . . umm . . . nontraditional circumstances. A year earlier, he, his wife Kasey, and Jaguars kicker Jaret Holmes all suffered serious burns when a hot fondue pot tipped over during an offseason dinner party at Hansen's house.

"We were just cooking in our kitchen and a pot overturned and spilled on our tile floor," Hanson told reporters.

The incident left the two players with first- and second-degree burns on their hands and feet, while Kasey took on second- and third-degree burns that required skin grafts and a two-week stint in the hospital.

Neither Hanson nor Holmes missed any time on the field due to their scaldings, but the lesson of these two situations became clear: Stay clear of Hanson when he is handling anything sharp or hot!

Weird, untimely injuries are nothing new to the game of football. In fact, one of the strangest happened in 1940 when Washington Redskins tackle Turk Edwards was on the field for the coin toss before a game against the New York Giants. After calling the toss and shaking hands with Giants great Mel Hein—the two men had been collegiate teammates at Washington State—Edwards turned to head back to his sideline and begin the contest.

That's when his cleat somehow got stuck in the grass. Edwards's pivot created enough torque to tear the ligaments in his knee. The injury didn't just end Edwards's game before it began, and didn't just end his season, but because of the nature of such injuries at the time and the lack of surgical reconstructions, it cost him his career. Edwards later became a coach for Washington and was elected to the Pro Football Hall of Fame in 1969 . . . but he never played another pro football game after that incident.

The field isn't always the most dangerous place for a football player. In 2007, after a win over the Eagles, Giants linebacker Chase Blackburn was in the locker room having just returned from a post-game shower. As he was cleaning his ears with a Q-tip, his arm was accidentally bumped by a reporter in the crowded area. The Q-tip was thrust deep into Blackburn's ear and nearly ruptured his eardrum. Blackburn dropped to the floor and said he lost hearing in the ear, which also began to bleed. Blackburn's hearing eventually did return in time for him to win the first of his two Super Bowl rings for the Giants later that same season.

Sometimes recovering from one injury can lead to an entirely new one.

In 2006, Steelers guard Kendall Simmons had hurt his foot in a game, and was icing it the next night while sitting at home watching *Monday Night Football.* The only problem was that he fell asleep during the game and the chemical ice pack he was using left a frostbite-like burn on his foot.

Simmons wound up missing the next week's game not because of the football injury, but because of the one from the ice pack!

The Washington Redskins decided to embark on a fun team-building field trip outing during offseason workouts in 2007. All their players went to participate in a paintball excursion. Not all of them returned in working order, however.

LaRon Landry, then a rookie safety, took a paintball shot to his groin that left him unable to participate in the team's minicamp that opened two days later. Ouch!

Whether or not the bullseye was an accident has never been proven, but there were reports at the time that Landry had hit one of his teammates during the course of a battle, knocking him out of the game, and when Landry approached the downed player to "finish him off," the teammate raised his own weapon and popped the rookie at point-blank range.

However it all went down, Landry was back on the field shortly after his recovery period and went on to have a successful career.

"It's kind of bizarre," Washington coach Joe Gibbs said at the time. "Almost anything can happen in life, so every now and then something like that does happen."

Kindal Moorehead hadn't even gotten on the field for his first NFL practice before he sustained a bizarre injury as a rookie for the Panthers.

On the opening day of Panthers training camp in 2003 in Spartanburg, South Carolina, Moorehead said he awoke with what he thought was a mosquito bite on his right forearm. It itched, but Moorehead thought it would go away eventually.

It did not.

Four days later, that right forearm, hand, and elbow had swelled. The team's medical staff sent him back to Charlotte for tests and he wound up in a hospital for four days fighting an infection.

"I was just looking at it like a regular bug bite," Moorehead told reporters at the time. "But then my arm kept swelling up. When I went to the hospital and they said they would have to keep me for a few days, then I started to get worried about it. Things like that happen that you have no control over."

The team eventually came to believe that Moorehead had been bitten by a spider in his sleep. Unlike the radioactive one that gave Peter Parker his superpowers, this one wound up costing Moorehead a few weeks of practice.

Quarterback Taylor Heinicke showed up at Vikings training camp in 2016 with a cast on his left foot after an offseason injury he'd suffered while breaking into a house.

His own house!

"I was locked out of my house after a late-night movie," Heinicke told reporters. "I came back and there's no one home, and I'm trying to nudge the door a little. It was one of those double doors. I thought it just needed a little nudge. Me and my buddy were getting it going a little, but when I put my foot to the door, my foot kind of slipped and it went through a window. It was just kind of a freak accident."

The incident resulted in a severed tendon, and Heinicke missed several months of action because of it.

Washington quarterback Gus Frerotte scored on a 1-yard run against the Giants in a 1997 game and celebrated in what he thought was going to be a "manly" way: by head-butting a "padded" wall just beyond the end zone.

Wrong move.

The quarterback wound up sustaining a sprained neck that required X-rays and a trip to the hospital for evaluations.

"You know, if you didn't have a sense of humor about it, I don't think that you would ever survive it," Frerotte said on a podcast nearly twenty years after the incident. "I don't think I go anywhere without somebody talking about it, or asking me about it, or what happened. And they try to be nice, but they really kind of want to be mean, some of the people. And other people just want to know what happened."

Frerotte returned to action the following week against the Rams, but broke his hip in that game and missed the rest of the season. But despite a very respectable career, it is his fight with the wall that most people remember most about his time in the NFL.

"It happened, and I've been able to move on from it, but I still can talk about it, because it was a part of my life," Frerotte said. "You know, it didn't define me, and it still doesn't define me. And that's what's great. I think if I didn't laugh about it, I wouldn't have been able to go on and play another ten years after that."

Seattle fullback Owen Schmitt was so pumped up when he came out onto the field before a 2009 game against the Jaguars that he smashed his own helmet against his noggin. Repeatedly. To the point where his face began to bleed all over his uniform.

The gash on his forehead required stitches, and the fullback had to swap out his blood-stained jersey for a cleaner one, but Schmitt was able to play in the game after a lecture from his coach.

"I said, 'Hey, pal, if you get hurt, we don't have anybody else,'" Seahawks coach Jim Mora told reporters afterward. "That's just his enthusiasm. He came over and apologized. I told him, 'Use your head.'"

Probably not the best-worded advice ever given. But hey . . . Schmitt happens!

Pro Bowl kicker Martin Gramatica's younger brother, Bill, made his NFL debut with the Cardinals in 2001. Less known for starting his career by nailing his first 16 of 20 field goals, Bill, like his brother, was known for "excessive" celebrations after hitting field goals, no matter the distance. Then, in a game against the Giants, Bill kicked a 43-yard field goal that gave the team three points. As the football sailed through the uprights, Gramatica leaped in the air and pumped his fist to celebrate. However, when he came back to the turf, he crumbled into a pile with a torn ACL. He would finish the game with another field goal and extra point, but his season was over after that.

Gramatica returned the following season and spent a total of four years in the NFL. And he did have a sense of humor about the incident for which he is best known... eventually.

"You guys got it wrong," he told reporters about a decade afterward. "You said I got hurt jumping. My jump was excellent. It was my landing I needed to work on."

Nate Burleson broke his arm in an act of heroism while trying to save . . . a pizza.

Prior to his prolific broadcasting career, Burleson was a wide receiver for the Lions and during the 2013 season—his last as a player—fractured his wrist in two places during a one-car accident on a Michigan highway.

"He had purchased two whole pizzas, and one was sitting on top of the other one, and I guess when he was driving one of them was slipping off, and he was reaching over to push it back onto the seat and overcorrected and hit the median wall," Michigan State Police Lt. Michael Shaw told ESPN of the incident. "It was actually a whole pizza."

Burleson missed seven games and the Lions, who were 3–0 at the time of the accident, finished the season with a 7–9 record. But when he did return to the field, Burleson celebrated his next touchdown by imitating a pizza delivery guy and serving the football to the fans in the crowd.

In 2020, when he was a co-host of *Good Morning Football* on the NFL Network, Burleson was asked to name the biggest regret of his career.

"Trying to save that pizza while driving," he said. "I'm dead serious. I swerved three or four times and remember getting out of the car to check my legs. There was a short sigh of relief when I realized my legs were fine, but that's when I noticed my arm was broken.

I looked down and remember saying out loud, 'I just messed up our season.'"

"Who knows how that season would've played out or how many more years I would've been in the league if it weren't for that deep dish pizza?"

"For the record, though, I still eat it all the time. I just have it delivered now."

Strange Stories, Part II

Elvis Grbac was named *People* magazine's Sexiest Athlete of 1998 . . . by mistake!

According to former *Sports Illustrated* writer Jeff Pearlman, the player the magazine *actually* chose was Rich Gannon, then a thirty-three-year-old quarterback for Kansas City who would lead the Raiders to a Super Bowl and win an MVP award a few years later. But when *People* sent a photographer to the Chiefs to take pictures of Gannon, they forgot to mention his name and said only he was the quarterback. The photographer wound up snapping dozens of frames of Grbac, Gannon's backup.

Grbac certainly wasn't hideous looking, but didn't quite fit the "sexy" mold *People* usually strives for in making such determinations the way Gannon did.

"The pictures made their way back to the New York offices, and editors were dumbfounded," Pearlman said. "This was their Sexiest Athlete? Yet upon learning the truth, no one with the magazine had the heart to tell Grbac that an unfathomable mistake had been made. As a result, Elvis Grbac reigns as *People*'s 1998 Sexiest Athlete."

The profile article's final line sums up the situation very well: "His personality makes him sexy."

Pearlman said editors at *People* would routinely ask folks from their sister publication, *Sports Illustrated*, for advice and suggestions on such matters.

"In 1998, for a reason I'll never understand, they decided not to seek out help."

After signing a $100-million contract in 2011, Texans defensive lineman J. J. Watt told late-night host Jimmy Kimmel he went home and googled "What do rich people buy?" The results, he said, all seemed too extravagant, so he didn't make any big purchases.

Lions head coach Dan Campbell is known for his feisty nature both in public and private. In 2021, his first year with the team, his players found out just how tough he can be.

"Coach was talking to a team meeting, he was getting all fired up, and his tooth flew out," quarterback Jared Goff recalled in a 2024 interview. "Like, one of his literal teeth flew out onto the ground. And without missing a beat, he just picked it up, put it back in, and just kept going on with his pretty intense speech he was giving us. And everyone's like "Did his tooth just fly out? What was that?" And he never talked about it. He never brought it up again and just kept it moving."

Bill Belichick's penchant for sage football advice in critical situations isn't always on the mark. Former Patriots punter Josh Miller recalled a conversation with his head coach during the waning moments of a tense Super Bowl XXXIX against the Eagles in Jacksonville.

"So here I am, with 20 seconds left on the field, and there's timeout after timeout after timeout. I'm sitting there on the field like, 'Jesus, this is not where I want to be right now.' So it was a long timeout, Belichick says, 'Miller, come here!' I'm like, 'What's up, Coach?' He's like, 'Listen, just get rid of the ball. I don't care where it goes.' I'm like, 'OK, fantastic, easy enough, I'll do that.' I'm running back onto the field. He's like, 'Miller, come here again! If you can get it inside the 10, that's obviously what we're looking for.' I'm like, 'OK.' And as I'm running back out, he's like, 'Forget it, listen, just get rid of the effing ball, please. Josh, just don't drop it.' I'm like, 'Don't drop it? That's what you tell me?' He was like, 'Yeah, that was dumb.'"

In a 2017 game against the Panthers, Green Bay linebacker Clay Matthews saw the formation and knew what was coming . . . at least he *thought* he knew.

"It's that wheel route! It's that wheel route!" he began yelling, alerting the tendency to his teammates.

Panthers quarterback Cam Newton heard him, too.

"You been watching film, huh?" Newton asked Matthews across the line of scrimmage. "That's cool. Watch this."

Newton then received the ball and threw a touchdown pass to Christian McCaffrey . . . and not on a wheel route.

When the Patriots (still of the AFL at the time) played at Nickerson Field in Boston against the Dallas Texans in 1961, an individual known as "the man in the trench coat" ran into the end zone and joined the Patriots' defense for the final play of the game. Security was lax enough that no one flinched, and he wound up in the middle of the play as Dallas snapped the ball. Not only that, but he managed to knock down a pass from Cotton Davidson that could have been the game-winning touchdown. The officials allowed it and the game ended in a Patriots victory and a celebration.

"All the fans rushed the field, and it was like everyone wasn't sure what they saw," Larry Eisenhauer, a Patriots defensive end on that team, would later say. "But we watched the film on Monday, and we saw this guy jump from the crowd and knock it down."

According to the *New York Times*, for years thereafter, Patriots owner Billy Sullivan, who was commonly seen in a London Fog–style trench coat, was rumored to be the Patriots' 12th man on the play. Famously, Sullivan never denied it.

Players get cut by teams for all kinds of reasons: performance, personality, financial implications. In 2013, the Broncos had to cut star linebacker Elvis Dumervil because of a late fax.

The team had wanted to keep Dumervil, and even negotiated a new contract with him in the days before the start of free agency. Everyone verbally agreed to the terms about 35 minutes prior to that deadline, but Dumervil, who was in Miami searching for a Kinkos, and his agent, who was in his office in Philadelphia, were unable to fax signed versions of the deal back to Denver. It eventually got there . . . but six minutes past the 4 p.m. cutoff time. It didn't matter by then because at 3:59, growing uneasy waiting for the document and facing a $13 million fine for exceeding the salary cap without the signed deal in hand, the Broncos were forced to waive Dumervil. He became a free agent and wound up signing with the Ravens . . . after firing his agent and, presumably, investing in a new fax machine.

In 1972, in the last game of the year, running back Dave Hampton became the first player in Falcons history to rush for 1,000 yards in a season when he took the ball for a 2-yard gain in the fourth quarter, giving him 1,001. The game against the Chiefs was momentarily stopped in celebration and Hampton was given the game ball to mark the achievement.

On the next possession, though, quarterback Bob Berry slipped while trying to execute a handoff. The skewed timing left Hampton with the ball and surrounded by Kansas City defenders. He was tackled for a 6-yard loss and wound up finishing the season with only 995 rushing yards.

One of the most memorable punt returns in Panthers history went for zero yards and was accomplished by the team's mascot, Sir Purr. In a 1996 game against the Steelers, Pittsburgh's Rohn Stark launched a kick. It bounced at the 4-yard line, trickled into the end zone, and was still very much a live ball that any of the Panthers players on the field could have scooped up and tried to return. Instead, Sir Purr was like a kitten with a ball of yarn and pounced on it.

The folks in the stadium loved it. The Panthers players gave Sir Purr high-fives, and even Steelers coach Bill Cowher was laughing. The referees, though, were not quite as amused. They initially threw a penalty flag on the Panthers (it was rescinded) and ruled the punt a touchback, and then chased down the mascot—who tried hiding behind the goalpost and various security officers—to give him a stern talking to about interfering with the action.

The 18–14 victory won the NFC West title for the Panthers and gave them a first-round bye in the playoffs, but on ESPN's highlights of the game later that night the most interesting nugget was this statistical credit in graphic form: "Sir Purr. Punt returns: One. Yards: Zero."

During their championship era, the tight-lipped Patriots were never known for their trash talking. That doesn't mean they didn't get their zingers in when they wanted to, though.

In 2011, before a playoff game against the Jets and head coach Rex Ryan (whose infatuation with feet had recently become embarrassingly public), New England receiver Wes Welker did some sole-searching and managed to squeeze eleven podiatric references into a mere nine-minute interview session with reporters. It included numerous references to players such as Darrelle Revis and Deion Branch having "great feet," about the Patriots wanting to put "our best foot forward," about players being "good little foot soldiers" and how in the playoffs "you can't just stick your toe in the water."

Asked about Ryan's blitz packages directly, Welker said: "You definitely have to be on your toes."

They were all mostly subtle clichés standing alone, but together they created a big heap of trouble for Welker, who was benched to start the game that the Patriots wound up losing.

It was worth it, though.

"Wes always brought a lot of life to things and he had a great personality, always keeping things light for everybody," Tom Brady said years later. "Who cares if it got him in trouble?"

SANCHEZ'S SILLY "SIGNATURE" MOMENTS

In 2009, the Jets were finishing up a 38–0 win over the Raiders in Oakland, and rookie quarterback Mark Sanchez was getting hungry. So he did what most people do at a ballpark when that happens: He bought a hot dog. Or, at least, he had a non-player on the sideline get one for him.

Unfortunately for Sanchez, the TV cameras caught him scarfing down the frank on the bench while the game was still going on, and the snacky quarterback had to apologize for his appetite.

"I wasn't feeling very good and didn't eat much before the game, so I was feeling a little queasy," he said. "Toward the end of the game, I probably should have eaten one of those bars or something, but someone offered [a hot dog], so I grabbed it and tried to be discreet about it, but obviously not discreet enough."

(Continued on next page)

It became one of the video clips that helped define Sanchez's tenure with the Jets. Until . . .

Thanksgiving Day, 2012, when the "Butt Fumble" was born.

Sanchez and the Jets were facing the Patriots on *Thursday Night Football*, with an estimated 20 million viewers tuning in. With his team down 20–0 midway through the second quarter, having already thrown an interception and being sacked once, Sanchez, trying to avoid another sack, scrambled and wound up running face-first into the backside of guard Brandon Moore, losing the football. It was recovered by New England's Steve Gregory and returned for a touchdown, but the slow-motion replays of Sanchez being jolted like a crash test dummy colliding with Moore's rear end provided the image that endures. The Patriots would go on to win, 49–19, in what the Jets (and Sanchez) hoped would be a game people would quickly forget. Unfortunately for them, the "Butt Fumble" took the top spot on *SportsCenter*'s "Not Top 10" list, where it would reign for forty weeks before being retired.

Jokey Jokes, Part IV

"You had some career," a fan once told Paul Paramount after he'd retired. "You have the most yards, most touchdowns, most catches, and most championships. Is there anything you can't do?"

"Actually," Paul said, "I wish I could listen to some music, but I can't."

"Why not?" the fan asked.

"Because," Paul said, "they told me I broke all the records."

Why did the fast wide receiver go scuba diving during the off-season? Because he liked to go deep.

Why didn't the dog want to play with the football? He was a boxer.

Which of Santa's reindeer is the best football player? Blitzen.

What NFL team did the rhino play for? The Chargers.

Why was the football team's flight delayed from landing? It was in a holding pattern.

What did the bee say after reaching the end zone? Hive scored!

When you hear someone go "Hut! Hut! Achoo!" you know what time of year it is: Football sneezin'!

Why didn't the nose make the football team? It wasn't picked by the coach.

Why do football players wear helmets on their heads? Because they won't fit on their feet.

What kind of player is best at giving change? The quarterback.

What kind of dog makes the best cheerleader? A Pom-Pomeranian.

Why is MetLife Stadium in New Jersey so cool and breezy? Because it is filled with Giant fans.

Comedian: "Want to hear a joke?
Quarterback: "No thanks. I'll pass."

Coach Flinty had a problem. His football players kept stealing the gear they were issued and supposed to return after practices. To combat it he had a set of shorts and shirts with "Property of Lawrence Taylor High School" printed on them. When those kept being taken, he changed the wording to "Stolen from Lawrence Taylor High School." Still, the shorts and shirts kept disappearing. Finally, Coach Flinty figured out how to stop the thieving. "Lawrence Taylor High School Fourth String" the next set of gear had written on it. He never lost a set again.

Star quarterback Danny Dunce wasn't allowed to play for the high school football team until his grades improved, particularly in English. Trying to complete an extra credit assignment he found himself wandering helplessly around the library.

"Can I help you?" the librarian asked.

"I hope so," Danny said. "I have to read a play by Shakespeare."

"Sure," the librarian said. "Which one?"

Danny looked at the shelves, thought for a moment, and said: "William."

Official-ly Funny Stories

Sometimes the funniest parts of a football game come from the officials, especially when they try to explain what the heck is happening on the field through their microphones.

Things got heated and very serious in a 1986 game between the Jets and Bills. Buffalo quarterback Jim Kelly threw a pass and was landed on by defensive lineman Marty Lyons. The two scuffled on the turf and teammates soon joined the ruckus as the sidelines cleared. Referee Ben Drieth was so infuriated by the violence he turned on his mic to describe the penalty on the play with one of the most inadvertently funny and now famous calls of all time. “After he tackled the quarterback he’s givin’ him the business down there,” Drieth said while throwing his own punches to demonstrate the infraction.

After going nearly the entire first half without a penalty flag in the 2013 Pro Bowl, Champ Bailey was called for a pass interference so blatant that it could not be ignored—even in that casual All-Star setting. The stadium cheered and laughed when referee Ed Hochuli began his description of the call with a comical clarification: "Yes, there are penalties in the Pro Bowl."

Hochuli became known not only as one of the more verbose NFL referees during his career, but one of the more buff ones as well. His well-defined arms and physique stood out even among the big, strong players. When the 2011 NFL lockout was coming to an end, Hochuli celebrated the return to action as only he would: "I got down on the floor and started doing pushups."

In a 2012 game between Washington and Pittsburgh, Steelers quarterback Ben Roethlisberger attempted a pass that hit official Darrell Jenkins in the face. Jenkins shook it off and the play was ruled an incompletion.

It's not only players and coaches who get scolded by referees. During a 1997 game between the Lions and Jets, the crowd was so loud at the Pontiac Silverdome that referee Dick Hantak threatened to dock a timeout or yardage from the Lions if their fans did not quiet down. "If the noise persists, the defense will be charged with a timeout," Hantak announced. When the Jets couldn't communicate at the line of scrimmage, Hantak sternly pleaded: "We insist that the crowd get quiet so we can get a play." The NFL abandoned its rules regarding crowd noise in 2007.

In a play that became known as the "Fail Mary" or the "Inaccurate Reception," Russell Wilson of the Seahawks threw a deep desperation pass to Golden Tate in the end zone on the final play of a game against the Packers. Because the NFL's officials were locked out at the time, the league was using replacement refs. The two officials near the play conferred and then simultaneously made separate signals, with Lance Easley raising his arms to signal touchdown and back judge Derrick Rhone-Dunn waving his arms for an incompletion. Chaos ensued as no one knew who had won the game. After a video review, the Seahawks were awarded the touchdown and the victory, but the league would later say that offensive pass interference should have been called to negate the score. The result was such a mess that Las Vegas estimated over $300 million in bets changed hands due to the final play. The NFL received a reported seventy thousand voicemail messages at its offices from angry fans. Even the President of the United State at the time, Barack Obama, weighed in, calling it a "terrible" situation and adding, "I've been saying for months, we've gotta get our refs back." Two days later, the league lifted the lockout and the regular officials returned to work.

That wasn't the only botched play by replacement officials. A few days earlier, Cowboys receiver Kevin Ogletree was wide open and cutting in the end zone when he slipped on a hat that a sideline official had inexplicably thrown onto the field. Tony Romo threw the pass in Ogletree's direction, but the receiver was unable to get up from his slip and make a play for it, costing the Cowboys a potential touchdown.

After a 2017 play, Raiders tight end Lee Smith pretended to jump up and head butt his friend Davon Godchaux of the Dolphins but was flagged for a personal foul. As referee Terry McAuley announced the penalty, Smith ran up to plead a case that was picked up by the open microphone: "I was just kidding around!" The penalty stood nonetheless.

As referee Jerome Boger was announcing a holding penalty called on Rams offensive lineman Harvey Dahl in a 2011 game against the Bengals, Dahl screamed, "That's not (bleeping) holding!" loud enough and close enough to Boger for it to be picked up by the referee's microphone so everyone in the stadium and everyone watching the game at home on television could hear him. Boger subsequently threw a second flag on Dahl for unsportsmanlike conduct. "I didn't know the microphone was on," Dahl said after the game. "My fault."

Boger has made his own gaffes, too. In 2022, his crew threw a flag against Seattle for sideline interference in a game with the Giants. He publicly explained that the foul was because, "the coaching staff of the Seattle Mariners was in the restricted area." The actual penalty was against the Seahawks, of course. The Mariners are Seattle's Major League Baseball team, and were most certainly not on the field.

Perhaps the "costliest" penalty flag ever thrown came in 1999, when referee Jeff Triplette tossed his on an offsides call . . . and it accidentally socked Browns offensive lineman Orlando Brown, sneaking between the bars of his facemask and hitting him in the right eye. The flag, as all were at the time, was weighted with BBs, and the hit temporarily blinded Brown. In 2001, Brown, who missed three seasons due to the injury, sued the NFL for $200 million, saying the flag incident prematurely ended his career. In 2002, he settled for somewhere between $15 million and $25 million. Today, nearly all penalty flags at all levels of football are weighted with sand and not those tiny but dangerous metal balls.

Outsiders' Perspectives

Funny football lines aren't limited to actual football participants. Throughout the years many outside observers have had plenty to say about the sport that led to smiles, laughs, and chuckles. Here are some takes that definitely come from worlds beyond the gridiron:

"I had pro offers from the Detroit Lions and Green Bay Packers, who were pretty hard up for linemen in those days. If I had gone into professional football the name Gerry Ford might have been a household name today."

—Gerald R. Ford, 38th President of the United States

"The reason women don't play football is because eleven of them would never wear the same outfit out in public."
—comedian Phyllis Diller

"The rules of football and the plot of *The Godfather* are the two most complicated things that every guy understands no matter how dumb he is."
—actor/comedian Julian McCullough

"Watching football is like watching pornography. There's plenty of action, and I can't take my eyes off it, but when it's over, I wonder why the hell I spent an afternoon doing it."
—author Luke Salisbury

"Football combines the two worst things about America. It is violence punctuated by committee meetings."
—political pundit George Will

"I don't think they have pads in my size. That's the only thing that has kept me from actually playing in an NFL game. I need petite."
—diminutive 5-foot-5 comedian Kevin Hart

"Baseball players are smarter than football players. How often do you see a baseball team penalized for having too many men on the field?"
—Major League pitcher Jim Bouton

"Sharks are as tough as those football fans who take their shirts off during games in Chicago in January, only smarter."
—writer Dave Barry

"When I went to Catholic high school in Philadelphia, we just had one coach for football and basketball. He took all of us who turned out and had us run through a forest. The ones who ran into the trees were on the football team."
—Basketball Hall of Famer George Raveling

"My dad didn't text me after the Patriots game, which is basically a Life Alert signal if you're from New England."
—comedian/writer Josh Gondelman

"It's weird. People say they're not like apes. Now how do you explain football then?"
—comedian Mitch Hedberg

"I prefer the tight yoga pants football players wear over the frumpy businesswoman slacks baseball players wear."
—writer and director Quinn Katherman

"I like football. I find it's an exciting, strategic game. And it's a great way to avoid conversation with your family at Thanksgiving."
—comedian Craig Ferguson

"It's weird that NFL players don't constantly look at their phones to check their stats."
—comedy writer Shawn Ries

"I'd catch a punt naked, in the snow, in Buffalo, for a chance to play in the NFL."
—Major League Baseball player Steve Henderson

"American football makes rugby look like a Tupperware party."
—British broadcaster Sue Lawley

"Anyone who thinks women talk too much has never sat through a six-hour Super Bowl pregame show."
—comedian Nora Barry

"The concussion protocol in 1988 was 'You good?'"
—comedian Gary Gulman

"Just remember, football is 80 percent mental
and 40 percent physical."
—Steve Emtman, *Little Giants*

"Anyone who's just driven 90 yards against huge men trying to kill them has earned the right to do jazz hands."
—late night host Craig Ferguson, on touchdown celebrations

"Thanksgiving dinners take 18 hours to prepare. They are consumed in 12 minutes. Halftimes of football games last 12 minutes. That is not a coincidence."
—writer Erma Bombeck

Comedian Jenny Slate admitted to not being a football fan in her Netflix special *Stage Fright*, although she did say she enjoys projecting her own sensibilities on the sport: "What I like to imagine is that the men have decided to be on a team, of course, because they're best friends. And they love to be best friends, and that's why they wear the same outfit. And they get together on a strict schedule and put on the same outfit and go rush after the toy. Oh my goodness, how darling!"

"He'll be the first quarterback in history to play three quarters and be able to bill them for four."
—*Tonight Show* host Jay Leno on Steve Young enrolling in law school in the offseason

"They do one-armed pushups so they can count with their other hand."
—Hall of Fame basketball coach Al McGuire on football players

FOOTBALL vs. BASEBALL

Comedian George Carlin had a legendary monologue regarding the difference between football and baseball. Among his observations:

"Baseball begins in the spring, the season of new life. Football begins in the fall, when everything's dying."

"Football has hitting, clipping, spearing, piling on, personal fouls, late hitting and unnecessary roughness. Baseball has the sacrifice."

He summed up his soliloquy by defining the two very different objectives of the sports:

"In football the object is for the quarterback, also known as the field general, to be on target with his aerial assault, riddling the defense by hitting his receivers with deadly accuracy in spite of the blitz, even if he has to use the shotgun. With short bullet passes and long bombs, he marches his troops into enemy territory, balancing this aerial assault with a sustained ground attack that punches holes in the forward wall of the enemy's defensive line. In baseball the object is to go home. And to be safe. 'I hope I'll be safe at home!'"

Jokey Jokes, Part V

Frankie Futile, the backup wide receiver, spent the whole game on the bench. Finally, as time was winding down, he went up to his coach.

"Knock, knock," Frankie said.

"Who's there?" the coach responded.

"Halibut."

"Halibut who?"

"Halibut you let me go in and play."

What do football players drink with their breakfast? Penal-tea.

What made the bad quarterback a bad comedian? Just like his passes, his jokes went over everyone's heads.

Did you hear about the Chicago player who had to have all his teeth pulled? He was a Gummy Bear.

Why was the football stadium packed with pigs? They all had skin in the game.

Why do eggs make good quarterbacks? They scramble very well.

Why did the coach trade his lazy running back for a dollar? Because he knew he could get four quarters out of a dollar.

Growing up, Patrick Mahomes always dreamed he'd become a star quarterback in the NFL. His prediction came to pass.

What do you get when you cross a football player with a rhinoceros? No one knows, but no one can stop it from scoring, either.

Which offensive linemen don't wear cleats? Centers. They wear hiking shoes.

What do you get when you cross an NFL running back with the Invisible Man? A talent like no one has ever seen.

What is the most suspicious play in football? The quarterback sneak.

Who are the most patriotic people on a football field? The referees. They always carry flags.

What did the seldom-used backup say when the team started charging him for his expensive first-class seat on the plane? Put me in coach.

Why didn't the football player want to go trick or treating? He was afraid he'd get penalized for a facemask.

What do both teams usually lose during a game? Their breath.

What does Tom Brady eat his cereal out of? Super Bowls.

Why did the football quit the team? It was tired of being kicked around.

Where do the ghosts watch the football games? Under the ghoul posts.

Why don't the Bears ever win when winter sets in? Because they are hibernating.

Why didn't Cinderella get any better at football? Because her coach was a pumpkin.

Clarence Clodpoll needed to talk to his coach right away and called him at home. The coach's wife picked up. Clarence explained the urgency of his request.

"I'm sorry, but he's not here right now," she said. "But I'll have him call you just as soon as gets in. What's your number?"

Clarence replied: "Seven."

Peter, a huge football fan, bought two tickets to a celebrity golf event crawling with famous football players. Stuck without a pal to go with, he brought along his wife, Sarah, who was not a sports fan at all. All of a sudden, in walked Peter's childhood hero and favorite quarterback of all time. He walked up to couple and introduced himself, as if that was even necessary.

"Hi," he said, extending his hand. "Joe Montana."

Peter was speechless. Sarah wasn't.

"Nice to meet you," she said. "I'm Sarah. New Hampshire."

One-Liners, Part II

"I want to rush for 1,000 or 1,500 yards, whichever comes first."
—George Rogers, former Saints running back

"I wouldn't ever set out to hurt anyone deliberately unless it was important—like a league game."
—Dick Butkus, Hall of Fame Bears linebacker

"I've been big ever since I was little."
—Bears defensive lineman William "Refrigerator" Perry

"If my mother put on a helmet and shoulder pads and a uniform that wasn't the same as the one I was wearing, I'd run over her if she was in my way. And I love my mother."
—Bo Jackson

Cardinals defensive end Darnell Dockett said he always read the nasty comments posted online about him and his team by 49ers fans. "They are really disrespectful, and I actually wish some of our fans would be like that sometimes, too."

"Everybody on that field has that alpha genetic that's like, 'Arrr, I'm tough.' But inside, you know, it's kind of like that 'Ohhh! Ohhh, geez!'"
—Panthers quarterback Cam Newton describing how it feels to take hard hits

After beating the Chargers in the 2013 playoffs, Broncos quarterback Peyton Manning was asked if he was looking ahead to facing Tom Brady and the Patriots in the AFC Championship Game the following week, and if retirement was in his thoughts following that season. "What's weighing on my mind is how soon I can get a Bud Light in my mouth after this win," he said.

"The first time I heard it, you know, I'm running out to the field and everybody's saying 'Cruuuuz!' and I'm thinking it's boos, and I'm

looking like, 'What did I do wrong? Is my zipper down?'"
—Giants wide receiver Victor Cruz on fans calling his name

"He treats us like men. He lets us wear earrings."
—University of Houston wide receiver Torrin Polk on the style of his coach, John Jenkins

"He couldn't spell cat if you spotted him the C and the T."
—Cowboys linebacker Thomas "Hollywood" Henderson describing Steelers quarterback Terry Bradshaw's intelligence

"I may be dumb, but I'm not stupid."
—Hall of Fame quarterback Terry Bradshaw's retort to Henderson

"Nobody in football should be called a genius. A genius is a guy like Norman Einstein."
—Redskins quarterback Joe Theismann

"The people don't take baths and they don't speak English. No golf courses, no room service. Who needs it?"
—Bears quarterback Jim McMahon, on traveling in Europe

"When you're rich, you don't write checks. Straight cash, Homey!" Hall of Fame receiver Randy Moss when asked how he planned to pay a fine from the league.

"People say I'll be drafted in the first round, maybe even higher."
—Running back Craig "Ironhead" Heyward, who wound up being selected in the first round (not sooner) by the Saints

"The NFL, like life, is full of idiots."
—49ers offensive lineman Randy Cross

Bob Golic, Cleveland Browns nose tackle, on what would happen if the National Football League ban on steroids was enforced: "There would be a lot of offensive linemen playing indoor soccer next year."

Prior to Super Bowl XVIII, played between the Redskins and Raiders, Washington lineman Joe Jacoby said that he would run over his own mother if it meant getting his hands on the Vince Lombardi Trophy. When asked for his take on Jacoby's comment, Matt Millen, a Raiders linebacker, didn't hesitate. "To win," he said, "I'd run over Joe's mom, too." Millen and the Raiders got the last laugh on that line with a 38–9 victory. Mrs. Jacoby, as far as anyone could tell, survived the game.

In a 2002 game against the Raiders, Chargers quarterback Drew Brees was hit with a water bottle thrown at him from the stands. "It might have been the hardest hit I took all day," he said, taking a jab at the Raiders' pass rush after his 27–21 overtime victory.

"For who? For what?" That's what Eagles running back Ricky Watters said at a 1995 press conference when asked why he didn't stretch out to try and catch a pass from Randall Cunningham that would have likely resulted in Watters getting drilled by a Tampa Bay defender. Watters would later say he regretted saying that selfish remark . . . but it didn't stop him from using it as the title of his autobiography!

In a 2011 appearance with David Letterman, Aaron Rodgers was asked what it was like being Brett Favre's backup for three years in Green Bay. "I was the guy who took all the reps during the offseason," Rodgers said, "and Brett was the guy who took all the reps during the season."

A center and linebacker in the AFL and NFL from 1961 to 1970, E. J. Holub went through numerous battles in the trenches and had over a dozen operations on his knees because of it. Discussing his medical history and the scars left from his playing days, Holub said: "My knees look like they lost a knife fight with a [little person]."

THE GOOSE IS LOOSE

Ahead of Super Bowl XXXV, Giants defensive end Michael Strahan was asked about Ravens oversized defensive tackle Tony "Goose" Siragusa.

"He'd have to amputate body parts to get to 340," Strahan said. "There have been times when Tony has run off the field and they've found chicken bones on the ground where he's been playing."

Strahan wasn't the only one to have some fun with Siragusa's dimensions. During a Ravens game against the Cowboys in 2000, the camera showed Siragusa on the sideline crammed into his equipment. Said John Madden: "The Goose either needs a little less head or a little more helmet."

Siragusa himself was known for some memorable lines, too.

(Continued on next page)

"If I wanted to learn a school song, I would've gone to Notre Dame or Penn State," he once said of his college choice. "I wanted to kill people on the football field. That's why I came to Pitt."

When he reported to a Ravens training camp and coach Brian Billick ordered everyone to be timed in a 40-yard dash, Siragusa refused the exercise. "If I have to run 40 yards in a game, we're in trouble," he told the coach.

And, in 2000, Siragusa suffered a spinal injury against the Titans that required him to be stretchered off the field and sent to shock trauma. He eventually returned to the game. "I guess I didn't want my boys to have all the fun out there," he said.

Jokey Jokes, Part VI

As the seconds ticked down in a very close game Donald Dizzy went running up to his coach on the sideline and handed him a long length of string.

"What's this for?" the coach asked.

Said Donald: "I thought it could help us tie the score."

How did the league punish the referee who kept making bad calls? They sent him to work on the chain gang.

Where did the cow quarterback go when he retired? Out to pass-ture.

What did the team of raindrops do before the football play? They puddled up.

What's the best way to keep the Ravens out of the end zone? Put up a scarecrow.

Where do defensive linemen spend their money during the off-season? At the tackle shop.

What is a football player's favorite dessert? Any given sundae.

Why don't judges ever get hurt playing football? Because they sit on the bench.

The library's football team had the best receivers in the league. They were book ends.

The receivers didn't lift weights Monday through Friday so on Saturday and Sunday they were weak ends.

What team doesn't wear any uniforms? The Chicago Bares.

Why did the candy bar get cut from the team after trying out as a receiver? It was a Butterfinger.

What do little sheep wear to get dressed up in Green Bay? Lamb bows.

What NFL team cooks the best food? The Kansas City Chefs.

Why did the coach start filling up the stadium with water? So he could send in the subs.

Why don't NFL players wear eyeglasses? Because football is a contact sport.

Which football player wears the biggest helmet? The one with the biggest head!

What do they charge for the corn at Tampa Bay football games? A buck-an-ear.

Why was the centipede banned from the football team? It took too long to tape his ankles.

Why was the pig thrown out of the game? He played too dirty.

What do you call a large reptile that leads the league in touchdowns? A dino-score.

Quarterback Mike Mercury took a huge hit and was knocked out. He lay on the turf until Dr. Dippy and the medical staff arrived. Frantic to assess the state of the player, the doctor grabbed his hand. "Can you hear me? Can you hear me, Mike?" he asked. "Squeeze my hand once for yes and twice for no."

Father Ernest had explained to the congregation many times that, as a Catholic, he would always root for Notre Dame in football, but that he also had a soft spot for the teams from where he grew up in Michigan. One day Notre Dame played Michigan State.

“Who are you rooting for in this one?” a parishioner asked him.

“I don’t know,” Father Ernest said. “I’m torn between Church and State.”

Coachspeak, Part II

Jets coach Rex Ryan held a late December press conference prior to a 2009 game against the Colts. "We're going to start with the injury report, obviously," he said before rattling off the names of the Indianapolis stars. "[Peyton] Manning, [Dallas] Clark, [Joseph] Addai, Reggie Wayne, [Dwight] Freeney, [Robert] Mathis, [Gary] Brackett, all those guys will not play." As the reporters were scribbling the "news," Ryan said: "Oh, hold up. That was my wish list for Santa Claus."

Ryan always had a grudge against Peyton Manning. Once he was asked about his defensive game plan for stopping the Hall of Fame quarterback when he was playing for the Broncos. "I'm not going to say we're going to poison his food or something, but that has crossed my mind."

Ryan also had plenty of run-ins with another Hall of Fame quarterback. In 2010, though, he said he felt a bond with him. "I never realized how similar that I am to Tom Brady," Ryan said in 2010. "I mean, the obvious physical appearance would be the first thing. The fact that he's married to a supermodel? Hello? Yeah, I'm also married to a supermodel." He grinned and held up a copy of *InStyle* magazine where his wife, Michelle, was featured in an NFL advertisement.

When a bad call against his Bengals prompted fans in Cincinnati to start throwing snowballs and beer bottles onto the field in 1989, coach Sam Wyche grabbed the public address microphone and chided them. "Will the next person that sees anybody throw anything onto this field, point them out and get them out of here? You don't live in Cleveland, you live in Cincinnati!"

Falcons head coach Jerry Glanville lamented the youth of his roster. "We had so many rookies this year, one of them asked me if we were going to a bowl game."

Glanville was also famous for leaving two tickets at the will call window for Elvis Presley at every game he coached. Asked if anyone ever claimed them he said: "I haven't heard from Elvis since his daughter married Michael Jackson. I think it killed him."

Asked by reporters about "going for a two" on the conversion after a late touchdown in a blowout win over rival Michigan in 1968, Ohio State coach Woody Hayes gave his reasoning: "Because I couldn't go for three."

Grouchy and stern, "Iron" Mike Ditka didn't always get along with his zany loose cannon quarterback of the Bears, Jim McMahon. Ditka offered a medical update on McMahon after a 1987 procedure. "The shoulder surgery was a success. The lobotomy failed."

Ray Perkins, the new coach of the Tampa Bay Buccaneers, was asked if his wife objected to his 18-hour workdays. "I don't know. I don't see her that much."

FAREWELL ADDRESSES

Coaches certainly don't last forever, and sometimes their parting words are their best lines.

"If you aren't fired up with enthusiasm, you will be fired with enthusiasm," Hall of Fame coach Vince Lombardi once said.

While he spelled out the acronym in several contexts, including aiming it at officials with whom he disagreed over various calls, Jerry Glanville said: "If you are a pro coach, NFL stands for 'Not For Long.'"

Bill Belichick used what was supposed to be his introductory press conference as head coach of the Jets in early 2000 to instead announce he would not be accepting the position. Told by the team that he couldn't just get out of his contract without formal documentation he grabbed a cocktail napkin and scribbled on it: "I resign as HC of the NYJ."

Frank Broyles, who was the athletic director at Arkansas, was asked if would still like football coach Ken Hatfield if he won only half of his games. "Sure I would. I'd miss him, too."

Perhaps the most succinct farewell, though, came from John Ralston in 1976. "I resigned as the Broncos coach because of illness and fatigue," he said. "The fans were sick and tired of me."

Jokey Jokes, Part VII

Not only was the football team at Rozelle High one of the worst in the state, but they also had terrible school spirit. It was so bad that at one of their games the cheerleaders were just sitting in the bleachers, their pom-poms on the ground, scrolling on their phones. Principal Patch saw them and chided them.

"Don't you think you girls should be down there cheering for your team?" she asked.

Without even looking up from her phone one of them replied: "No. I think we should be down there playing for our team."

Frankie Frugal bought the cheapest seat in the house for the big game and then kept an eye out for any open ones. Shortly before kickoff he found the perfect spot, right in the front row at the 50-yard line. He snuck down and asked the man sitting next to it if the seat was taken.

“No,” the man said. “I used to come to every game with my wife, but ever since she passed away, I’ve had to come alone.”

“Why don’t you just invite a friend?” Frankie asked.

“I tried,” the man said. “They are all at her funeral today.”

Why did the rookie football player go to the bakery? He wanted to become a roll model.

What is Drew Brees’s favorite show? *Game of Throws*.

Why did the football player go to the therapist? He needed help tackling his issues.

Why did the football team bring a shovel to the game? To bury the competition.

What is a dog’s least favorite football play? The flea-flicker.

Why did the receiver have a GPS installed in his helmet? To help him find better routes.

Why does a moon rock taste better than a football? Because it is a little meteor.

What did one football helmet say to the other? You stay here, I'll go on ahead.

Having lived a long, happy life, Tom Brady arrives in heaven and God is there to show him around. God shows Brady the park where people play football all day every day. He shows Brady the ocean where people swim and frolic. He shows Brady the library that has film and breakdowns of every football play ever designed. Brady is overjoyed.

Then God shows Brady where he'll be living. It's a cozy, comfortable, three-bedroom home. Over the doorway are seven subtle stars to signify Brady's Super Bowl titles. On the neat front lawn is a flagpole, and at the top of it waves a small banner with Brady's number 12.

"I think I'll like it here," Brady says.

God and Brady then walk around the neighborhood a little further and they come across a lavish mansion situated on several acres of garden-like property. It is a blue house with a huge Giants "NY" logo painted on the roof next to the helicopter pad. Next to the garage is a yacht, also blue, also showing the Giants logo, with the number "10" painted on it. The hedges out front have been shaped into two towering Lombardi Trophies. There is, of course, a flagpole. It waves an oversized banner that can be seen for miles and miles that says "Manning."

Brady is a little taken aback.

"God," he says, "I don't mean to sound ungrateful but, I mean, I am the greatest quarterback of all time. How come Eli gets a much nicer house than I have?"

"Oh, that's not Eli's house," God says. "It's mine."